T0381368

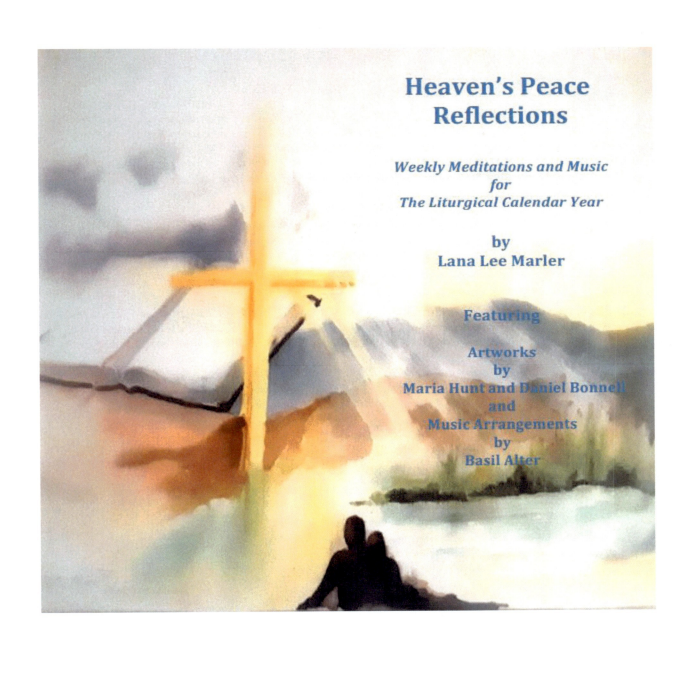

Heaven's Peace Reflections

*Weekly Meditations and Music
for
The Liturgical Calendar Year*

by
Lana Lee Marler

Featuring

Artworks
by
Maria Hunt and Daniel Bonnell
and
Music Arrangements
by
Basil Alter

WestBow Press books may be ordered through booksellers or by contacting:

WestBow Press
A Division of Thomas Nelson & Zondervan
1663 Liberty Drive
Bloomington, IN 47403
www.westbowpress.com
844-714-3454

Because of the dynamic nature of the Internet, any web addresses or links contained in this book may have changed since publication and may no longer be valid. The views expressed in this work are solely those of the author and do not necessarily reflect the views of the publisher, and the publisher hereby disclaims any responsibility for them.

Book Front Cover Art: *Heaven's Reflection* by Daryl Rojas
Book Back Cover Art: *Sky Promise* by William Marler
Title Page Art: *The Sabbath* by Maria Hunt

ISBN: 978-1-6642-9401-1 (sc)
ISBN: 978-1-6642-9402-8 (e)

Library of Congress Control Number: 2023904068

Print information available on the last page.

WestBow Press rev. date: 02/06/2024

In Dedication

to

Rev. Dr. James "Jim" A. Townsend

and

Dr. Lucy Forsyth Townsend

for

Love and Prayers, Encouragement

and

Scholarly Support in My Writing Endeavors

A Word of Special Thanks

to

Maria Hunt

and

Daniel Bonnell

for

Generosity of Spirit and Collaboration

in this Labor of Love

In Gratitude

To Dr. Robert G. Lee, my namesake and childhood pastor,
For leading me to faith in Christ and believer's baptism;
Thank you for the image I have of you
kneeling beside the pulpit each Sunday morning
in prayer and humility before you preached.

To The Rev. L. Noland Pipes, Jr.,
Pastor, Priest and Mentor in my adult faith journey;
You have been a *Father* to me in the church and like my *father*
since my earthly father went to heaven.
Thank you for teaching me faithfulness
and how to encourage others.

To The Rev. Dr. Stephen H. Cook,
Pastor, Constant Friend and Brother in Christ
Thank you for being a living example of *The Good Shepherd*
To all those lambs in God's flock you are called to serve
and for your unwavering support for the ministry
of this particular handmaiden of the Lord.

Contents

*Album Music Hyperlink https://heavens.jacobsladdercdc.org/

Heaven's Peace
by Lana Lee Marler

Please come and sing along with me of the Great Redeemer's Love.
How long before the earth was formed, He claimed us all by His dear blood.
With hands giv'n sworn to help and heal, and eyes and heart compassionate;
Our Lord Creator lived as we, yet pure in all His ways.

It is with humble, grief strick'n hearts,
That we bow before the One; The Lord Who came to give Himself
A ransom once for all. Our sins remembered no more,
Having been washed in His blood, ensure that in God's love,
Evermore, our lives will be restored.

So let us join in one accord to honor and praise His name;
And seek to live, love and serve this world He came to save.
Always looking to our Lord for His power and His grace;
Until in His good plan we find ourselves
All gathered in Heaven's peace.

https://heavens.jacobsladdercdc.org/home/peace

Preface

Books can be a problem. Not just in their content, but because some of us simply love them too much. I am an admitted bibliophile with bulging shelves and scattered stacks here and there - some read, some partly read, some representing hope for the future. One thing is clear. My reading habits improve when I exercise a little discipline and take one bite of the apple at a time lest another half- finished core join the stack.

This admission is offered as a partial explanation for my admiration of Lana Lee Marler's "Heaven's Peace Reflections." Lana offers us a rich feast in small bites. Beyond that, she offers us more than reflections prompting thought and feeling. She invites a larger reflection through music and art. This collection offers us the opportunity to open eye, ear, and heart and to be enriched as the three become a mutual blessing to the beholder.

To elaborate the reference to a feast of small bites, this book will join "New Morning Mercies" by John David Tripp and "A Year with C. S. Lewis" edited by Patricia Klein as books that offer me a gospel feast in one course and require but a few minutes from a daily schedule.

There is an added bonus for those Christians who worship in liturgically oriented churches and follow the Christian year with its seasons, feasts, fasts and special days. I would urge you to open to the Contents page and observe this manner of focusing our personal as well as congregational worship. It has served countless generations of Christians as we attempt to faithfully follow in the footsteps of our Lord.

Finally, although there are subjects and themes which repeat time and again, there is no lack of variety. Lana is often responding to immediate circumstances and observations through the eyes of faith. Her story becomes His story. May your story be wonderfully enriched by *hers* and *His*.

The Rev. L. Noland Pipes, Jr., Retired

Mary in Her Ninth Month by Daniel Bonnell

Season of Advent
The Longing by Lana Lee Marler

When will it stop - the pain of this longing? Seeming without beginning or
ending. Standing or sitting, lying or sleeping; This ever-present longing.

Inside and out, my soul's tears are falling. It's me and *not* - close but far - this
longing. Glimpsing does not permit the heart's holding;
Nor a brushed cheek soothed from aching.

All those who do not know this longing, Pity me not, my life thus disgracing;
For this poor heart would spend itself wandering
Down paths sure to find it embracing.

What kind of peace inhabits this longing? Husbanded by great toil and striving.
Not an easy peace won in the struggling,
But peace without which there's no living.

All those who do not know this longing, Pity me not, my life thus disgracing;
For this poor heart would spend itself wandering
Down paths sure to find it embracing.

Therefore, I'll cling to this blanket of longing, So long as my heart beats 'neath
its swaddling. Where it takes me is not for the caring;
Just to know and be known - the journey sharing.

https://heavens.jacobsladdercdc.org/home/longing

Cold feet…Having done all to stand

"Baby, it's cold outside" but it is also cold inside! It is after all that time of year, but truth be told - having "cold feet" is not always determined by the weather. "Cold feet"…what does that idiom mean? My husband would tell you right quickly that having cold feet thrust up against him under the blanket on a cold winter night was not part of the marriage vows. Regarding "cold feet" the believer's vows to God are a different matter. The origin of the phrase is a matter of debate but suffice it to say that to have "cold feet" is a descriptive metaphor about being too fearful to undertake or complete an action. An applicable one at that, since we can certainly agree it is difficult to walk or even balance your weight on feet that are severely cold.

From time to time, as members of the human race, all of us experience feelings of apprehension and doubt which serve to paralyze our actions. Instead of running to God in faith, we run and hide-out in the darkness of fear and unbelief. Biblical stories of our ancestors in the faith, such as Moses, Abraham, David and the apostle Peter reveal the human condition of being "frozen" and unable to move in faith due to fear.

Ephesians Chapter 6 (ESV) casts a warm light on the "cold feet" metaphor: "Finally, be strong in the Lord and in the strength of his might…Therefore take up the whole armor of God, that you may be able to withstand in the evil day, and having done all, to stand firm…and, as shoes for your feet, having put on the readiness given by the gospel of peace." How do we manage our "cold feet" and put on the Godly shoes given by the gospel of peace?

One possible answer to this challenge is the prayer of faith. We sang a rousing old gospel favorite at our mid-week service known as "Standing in the Need of Prayer." This is a beloved song but if you think about it, our postures of praying may not be standing but more often sitting or on our knees, even lying prostrate in a sick bed. The "need" of prayer in our lives is, of course, always there…So why does the song use the posture of "standing?" Perhaps the need for prayer co-exists with the notion of being frozen in fear with "cold feet" and unable to move in faith.

The Bible says in 2 Timothy 1:7: "For God has not given us a spirit of fear but of power and of love and of a sound mind." Let us confess our weakness for "cold feet" and remember to revel in the notion of standing in the need of prayer and having done all to stand firm in resolve to move in faith, be of sound mind and open heart to the power of the love of God given to us in Christ Jesus. May it be so with God's help!

Reflections

_____

_____

_____

_____

_____

_____

_____

It's so easy not to try...
It's not so easy not to cry.

Recently we made a road trip out west and visited Little Bighorn National Battlefield, an historical monument to pain, loss and suffering. Needless to say, we were profoundly impacted – the sad spirit on the land was unmistakable. The first person we met at the entrance was Park Ranger Janice Knowstheground (English translation), the family name of her father, a member of the Crow Indian tribe. There was a commitment to goodness and truth in her spirit but a residual hardship of sadness as well. To say her family "knowstheground" is not an understatement – she committed herself to honor what she knows as the work of her life.

It brought to my mind the life of Mary Magdalene, sometimes known as Mary of Magdala, who became one of the earlier followers of Christ and traveled along with Him. One can only assume that her life had been one of hardship – nothing is mentioned in scripture about her life and background as a Jewish girl from Magdala other than she had been a prostitute and possessed by seven demons, the exorcism of which was granted by Jesus (Luke 8:1-2 CSB). From that time forward, Mary Magdalene left whatever her life had been, following and supporting Jesus in His ministry through His crucifixion, death and resurrection. She was present at His empty tomb and witnessed that fact to the amazement of the other disciples (John 20:14-17 CSB). Scripture does not tell us of Mary's own ministry to the truth of what she lived, learned and witnessed after these events took place but one cannot deny that the core of her spirit would ever reflect its Light to the world.

Like the song from the animated movie "Return of the King" says, "It's so easy not to try" when life has exacted mental, physical, emotional and psychological hardships which cannot be explained and hardly justified. Perhaps you remember a female character from the movie, "Dances with Wolves" known as "Standswithafist". I, myself, have had an affinity with that name over the years in an effort to protect myself from harm or to stand my ground. In a world full of abuse and unfairness, why commit yourself to anything other than yourself?

Just as Indian Crow Park Ranger Janice Knowstheground has a name of description and definition, it would be noteworthy for all of us to adopt a similar tradition as we reflect on our lives before God the Creator and Savior of all people. Mary of Magdala became known as Mary Magdalene meaning reformed prostitute. In the Crow tradition, her name in translation would definitively be Mary "FollowerofChrist." Instead of the name "Standswithafist," I likewise, want to live a life as defined by the name, Lana "FollowsChrist".

It's so easy not to try", but It's 'not' so easy 'not' to cry over the grief, pain and suffering in a world that Christ gave his life to save while we, at times, huddle safe and protected in the shadows by unenlightened human tradition. May the Lord grant us courage to cast aside unworthy tradition and write our names anew each day by living our lives in honor of the "One" who truly "Knowstheground." Amen.

Which comes first?
The chicken or the egg…
Perspective or Perception

"I will lift up mine eyes unto the hills, from whence cometh my help. My help cometh from the Lord, which made heaven and earth" (Ps. 121:1-2 KJV) is our scripture verse of choice while travelling over or through the mountains – either by air or car. Each mode of transportation provides a unique opportunity for exploration but traveling by car has become our hands-on favorite because it is just that…hands-on. Peering out the window of an airplane offers a breathless view of the terrain above and below, but there is an intimacy absent in the journey.

Driving through mountain ranges – over steep cliffs and then spiraling down again into deep ravines and slot canyons, one is consistently visually challenged to look upward or downward at each curve in the road. What you see and therefore experience depends on this changing visual perspective which results in your journey being internalized. One's perception of the vastness of nature's bravado is not impacted by the altitude or stature of the observer. Whether hang gliding or walking, "up is still up" and "down is still down."

Not so, for the "wee", albeit rich, tax collector known as Zacchaeus in gospel accounts such as found in Luke 19:1-10 NIV. When Jesus was passing through Jericho, Zacchaeus was curious to see Him, but the crowds and the tax collector's short stature prevented him from getting even a hasty glance. The Sycamore tree was handy, and Zacchaeus was able, so like a bird, he established a perch in the tree looking down to the street below and waited for the Savior to pass. Zacchaeus' presence did not go unnoticed, however, as Jesus looked up when passing the tree and admonished Zacchaeus (by name) to come down so that he could host the Lord in his house.

Zacchaeus' downward observation of Jesus was not merely thus – It became a perspective that was transformative. He altered his position in several ways…He came down from his "high" perch in the tree (both literally and figuratively), welcomed Jesus, confessed his transgressions and made public restitution. As a consequence of Jesus upward gaze and acknowledgement of the man (Zacchaeus) and his need, salvation came to reside in his house and heart forever as proclaimed by the Lord Himself. "'For the Son of Man came to seek and to save the lost.'" (Luke 19:10 NIV)

This gospel account is testimony to the fact that "perspective precedes perception." Zacchaeus saw a stranger become Savior and Jesus saw a sinner become saved by grace. Whether from exalted status or face-down in the dirt in society, our vantage point is always looking up at the cross of Christ, whose gaze upon the lost He came to save is forever transformative. As believers and receivers of grace, may we share Christ's loving perspective of the world so that the perception of the world is to see the "Truth" of the crucified Christ and thus receive His salvation. (As far as the chicken and the egg – God made them both! Perspective precedes Perception)

Reflections

_____

_____

_____

_____

_____

_____

_____

_____

_____

_____

_____

_____

_____

_____

_____

_____

Reflections

The still small voice, When small is anything but…

One of the most influential American writers of the 20th century, Kurt Vonnegut, Jr. is noted for saying, "Enjoy the little things in life because one day you`ll look back and realize they were the big things." Elijah of the Old Testament would agree with the assertion of this 20th century novelist, as would most of humanity. It is the memories of the details attached to the momentous events in our lives that immortalize them in our hearts.

One should take note the heading of this Sharing: "When small is anything but…" The only account in scripture of the "still small voice" is found in I Kings 19:11-13 KJV: "And he said, 'Go forth, and stand upon the mount before the Lord. And, behold, the Lord passed by, and a great and strong wind rent the mountains, and brake in pieces the rocks before the Lord; but the Lord was not in the wind: and after the wind an earthquake; but the Lord was not in the earthquake: And after the earthquake a fire; but the Lord was not in the fire: and after the fire a still small voice. And it was so, when Elijah heard it, that he wrapped his face in his mantle, and went out, and stood in the entering in of the cave. And behold, there came a voice unto him, and said, 'What doest thou here, Elijah?'

Why is this the single reference in the Bible of the "still small voice? The "still small voice" is contrasted to grandiose powers as in the strong wind, the earthquake, and fire. God speaks to us in tender fashion according to our need, especially when enduring the bombardments of life, as human beings the Glory of The Almighty would indeed be overwhelming. It is my belief that the "still small voice" of God is unique for each person – lovingly spoken in such a way so as not to be mistaken for any other voice and thus its concern and instruction is distinctively personal and healing. "Whispering Hope, written by Septimus

Winner in 1868 begins: "Soft as the voice of an angel, Breathing a lesson unheard; Hope with a gentle persuasion, Whispers her comforting word."

In modern translations, the phrase "still small voice" found in I Kings 19:11-13 KJV, is referred to it as "the sound of a low whisper" (ESV). In my own life, writing Sunday Sharing's is not something I just sit down and decide to do – I must wait upon God to reveal to me the topic and points of illustration. More often than not, His "still small voice" enters my consciousness in the late-night hours as I lie in the quiet on my pillow…And it is a voice I actually hear internally. I have found it to be frustrating and a futile waste of time and effort to endeavor to write a Sharing if I don't wait on the Lord for His gentle "whisper" of counsel. By His grace, may we always be attentive to the "Holy Whisper" of our Omnipresent Creator God.

Reflections

Christmas Eve
Even So, Come
by
Lana Lee Marler

Come, Lord Jesus; Come, Lord Jesus.
In the hush of the trembling stillness,
So silent are your gentle stirrings
On the scattered straw.

O Come, Lord Jesus; Come, Lord Jesus.
In this moment, scarcely can I breathe,
So sweet is your breath born
In the stable of this poor heart.

Even so, Come.

https://heavens.jacobsladdercdc.org/home/even

Stand and Deliver! "Mary, did you know?"

There are several meanings to the phrase: "Stand and Deliver." The most popular usage might be familiar to you from movies or literature set in the eighteenth century when highwaymen ordered unsuspecting travelers to halt and demanded they turn over any valuables. A more contemporary meaning is for a person to stand firm and perform his/her duties to the best of their abilities.

A lovely young friend of mine recently had her first child. A midwife was engaged so it was possible for the baby to be born at home…a pertinent story for this Christmas season, although the home-born infant was a little girl. When I heard the good news of my friend's home-born baby, it was easy for my thoughts to drift to the story of Mary, the mother of Jesus. Scripture gives no details of Mary's birthing of the Christ, but there is a song which casts its light, "Mary, did you know?" written by Mark Lowry in 1984. We do know that it was Jewish custom for a midwife to be present and provide assistance. Whether or not that was the case, Mary did not know, or indeed anticipate, the circumstance she would face that starry night so far from home…Nor did she have the wherewithal to flee the rustic stable and its inhabitants in search of comfort.

What we do know is that Mary answered the call to "stand and deliver." Until modern times, the means of birthing a child had been one of two ways with the assistance of midwives: 1) Either to stand holding on to a tree or board frame or 2) To position oneself over a birthing stool which had a hole in the bottom with soft cushioning underneath. Regardless of mode, Mary was faithful to "stand

and deliver," not only in the physical act of giving birth but also standing firm in conviction performing her duties to the best of her ability. The first chapter of Luke reveals the virgin Mary's response to the angel Gabriel's annunciation…"And the angel said unto her, 'Fear not, Mary: for thou hast found favour with God. And, behold, thou shalt conceive in thy womb, and bring forth a son, and shalt call his name Jesus…The Holy Ghost shall come upon thee, and the power of the Highest shall overshadow thee: therefore also that holy thing which shall be born of thee shall be called the Son of God.' And Mary said, 'Behold the handmaid of the Lord; be it unto me according to thy word.'"

"For unto us a child is born, unto us a son is given. (Isaiah 9:6 KJV)

The season of the ultimate gift is once again upon us. We know from scripture that Gabriel told Mary that she was highly favored of God. It seems accurate to assume that those whom God highly favors, He then enables to answer the call to do His will. None of us could imagine the faith and fortitude it required of Mary, the mother of Jesus, or of Christ, the human-born divine Son of God sent to give His life as Savior of the world. As His children, saved by grace, we do know that God will enable us to answer His call on our lives and say, "Be it unto me according to Thy word." To be the starry lights which shine in the darkness of night in this world, it is needful to "stand and deliver." With God's help in His plan of love and life for all creation, may we find ourselves likewise faithful.

Season of Christmas

Christmas Day

The Life of the Party
Knock, knock…
Who's there?
Merry? Or Mary?
No, it can't be Merry at my door when I feel so
Alone…At home…At work…In the car…In an elevator…
In bed at midnight…
With my thoughts…My fears…Nothingness…
More so than emptiness.
What is shaking…Is it me? Is this a panic attack?
The gift is waiting, likewise trembling at the door…
It is the Virgin's Child offering redemption and peace…
I open the door and rejoice to receive the gift of Love.
Thanks be to God…but I feel more like Mary than Merry.

In the pink…The sun will come up tomorrow

A new day…a new year…celebrations abound worldwide. So, why does a tinge of sadness swarm 'round me in the midst of all the gayety and glee? I must confess that change has never set well with me - feelings of insecurity, not unlike earth tremors, impact my soul where change is concerned. One would assume that change for the better would be a welcomed gift. That being the case for me, however, does not erase the inherent problem in my nature (and perhaps yours as well) of being strong-willed and desirous to be in control of my life.

Poised at the juncture of facing the prospects of a new year with all its indeterminate joys and sorrows, gains and losses, provides an opportunity for a time-out "so to speak." We know from scripture Luke 5:16 nkjv how the Lord Jesus made it common practice to withdraw from the chaos, demands and distractions of life and flee to the desolation of wilderness, so that time spent in prayer alone with God would grant Him strength and perspective.

Jesus' commitment to time-outs were not ends unto themselves but rather, a means to an end. His retreats of solitude were *designed* to prepare for future ministry - not punishment as our contemporary usage of the phrase "time-out" implies. The gospel of Mark 1:12 reveals Christ was driven by the Spirit into the wilderness in preparation for forthcoming trials - driven by The Light from light of day into darkness…only to emerge from that dark wilderness by design of The Spirit of Light back into the light of His ministry to those He came to save - from "the light to the light." Which brings me back to the issue of my fear of change - By God's grace I have learned that I am not God and garner no control whatsoever over my life. I wrote a song in testament to this revelation:

There is No I in You
by Lana Lee Marler

You lay me down to sleep And keep the soul of your lost sheep. Eyes close to the silent rhythm of each breath so serenely giv'n.

(Refrain)
There is no I in You. All that I have, I receive.
You alone are God and ever shall be. There is no I in You.

You own the terror of the night and the darkness our souls breathe in; But Your love abides in the hopes and dreams we believe in. (Refrain)

Because there is no I in Your death's dark dream shall not prevail; The waking song of all is that Your love never fails. (Refrain)

Coda
I am not God, neither can I be.
There is no I in You.

https://music.youtube.com/watch?v=SbrOcIspQ6c

The waking song of all tomorrow morning is that God's love never fails…the sun will come up tomorrow on a new day of a new year – the sky will be tinged pink with hope and not sadness – Thanks be to God for He alone is God.

2nd Sunday after Christmas
A Prayer for the New Year

Prayer to the Holy Spirit
Traditional Native American Prayer
Translated by Lakota Sioux Chief Yellow Lark in 1887
Music by Lana Lee Marler

O Great Spirit, Whose breath gives life to the world,
And Whose voice is heard in the soft breeze:
We need Your strength and wisdom.
Cause us to walk in beauty.

Give us eyes ever to behold the red and purple sunset.
Make us wise so that we may understand what You have taught us.
Help us learn the lessons You have hidden in every leaf and rock.

Make us always ready to come to You with clean hands and steady eyes,
So when life fades, like the fading sunset,
Our spirits may come to You without shame. Amen

https://heavens.jacobsladdercdc.org/home/prayer

Epiphany
by
Lana Lee Marler

Peering…pathless…

Lidless eyes searching the night of self.

Leering…jeering…

Lying eyes shunning the bright darkness.

Blinded, bound and gagging…gazing;

Hoping…hopeless…the gaze…met;

And longing…longed-for…

The lamps of the soul…lit.

https://heavens.jacobsladdercdc.org/home/epiphany

Reflections

_____

_____

_____

_____

_____

_____

_____

_____

_____

_____

_____

_____

_____

_____

_____

Befuddled?
Head to the huddle

Befuddled, meaning to be confused or perplexed, is a word not used in common discourse these days. This word, however, does have routine application in outreach ministry, when faced with the challenges of dealing with others and not knowing how to think clearly about certain situations. That is, how does the person in ministry answer the perpetual liar, drug user and thief trying to gain a daily hand-out? We "know" the person's agenda and we "know" that they are aware of the fact that we "know" that they are seeking provision without repentance or change in behavior. How can truth be shared, and successful ministry be accomplished in the reality of these competing agendas?

Whether to persons in your own neighborhood, impoverished areas of the city, family members, business, educational, professional and even charitable institutions, all ministry involves people who may or may not think or behave the same as those persons who are seeking to do ministry. An ever-present quandary at best, but one which does not have an unanswered question…The answer to the question above - Befuddled? can be found in N.T. Scripture regarding the early church:

Acts 2:42-47 NIV: "They devoted themselves to the apostles' teaching and to fellowship, to the breaking of bread and to prayer. Everyone was filled with awe at the many wonders and signs performed by the apostles. All the believers were together and had everything in common. They sold property and possessions to give to anyone who had need. Every day they continued to meet together in the temple courts. They broke bread in their homes and ate together with glad and sincere hearts, praising God and enjoying the favor of all the people. And the Lord added to their number daily those who were being saved."

We have all heard the saying "opposites attract" and we can attest to this tenet's validity in life. However, the converse may be true as well, in that "opposites detract," particularly in regard to working and teaching others whose lives and backgrounds are so dissimilar to our own. The saving grace in these situations is that "truth" is the hand-out - the Truth of God as revealed in Christ is not open to interpretation and the Truth never changes - those to whom the gospel has been shared will either accept or reject it. But those persons sharing the "truth" are imperfect sharers as are those who are potential receivers. Neither were the disciples perfect - each with varying issues and backgrounds, even though they were called to serve the people Jesus gave His life to save. The gospel of Mark tells us there were times the disciples misunderstood Jesus, showed lack of faith, were possessive, competitive, jealous, ambitious and hard-hearted. Moreover, when Jesus was arrested and taken away, they fled in fear. The truth of this narrative strikes close to home for all of humanity.

That being the case, one thing is imperative - When confused and perplexed while endeavoring to implement the ministry of the Kingdom of God, we must not forsake the assembling of ourselves together. We need to "huddle-up" with other believers in pursuit of God's wisdom and understanding as we fellowship and share in the "huddle" of the church or wherever that space might be. "For where two or three are gathered together in my name, there am I in the midst of them." Matthew 18:20 KJV.

Let's answer the call: "Huddle up!"

Let It Be So

The Lord Jesus tends His sheep. Laying down His life once for all;
There is no wash, rinse, repeat. A rule of His Kingdom to which I belong;
When I am weak, then I am strong.

These are hard times…But I woke up this morning; Showers continue…Showers of blessing will I receive this and every day: May God be with us in the rain He sends on the just and the unjust. "It will be worth it all when we see Jesus" but 'when' is now in God's perspective. We've all heard the saying, "Better late than never" but with God there is "no hurry and no delay." His timing is perfect because He is not constrained by time.

The question facing us… "Are we going to be people of faith or people in fear?" This has been a time of renewed fears over many things: life-threatening disease, economic ruin, war, downfall of morality and spirituality and even the banning of books. For all the books banned over the decades, the most banned book of all is the Bible. Thanks be to God that His Word Is! It has endured and will endure for our good and His glory.

What a wondrous time is this! " What wondrous Love is this!" The weather outside is frightful or not…but God's love is always delightful. So as long as He loves me so…Let it be so; Let it be so; Let it be so.

Grumbling…Rumbling
A Cautionary Tale

From time to time, most people find themselves complaining about circumstances. We often exclaim: "I'm dealing with a lot right now!" Even if we don't articulate it to others, the grumbling in our spirits leaks a perpetual rumbling which colors the landscapes of our lives. On our roadways there are yellow double lines of caution - coupled in recent years with rough patches in the asphalt - as "wake-up" calls when we venture into the oncoming lanes of traffic.

We have witnessed many "cautionary tales" in our lives with family, friends, work and church settings about the consequences of grumbling gone unaddressed. Our own stomachs "rumble" to communicate the body's need for nourishment. The scriptures are rife with historical instances of humans complaining, i.e., The Garden of Eden, the Israelites led by Moses in the desert, Jesus' disciples and church leaders vying for positions of power, to name a few. Scripture warns about crossing the yellow lines into grumbling and complaining: (I Peter 4:9 NKJV) "Be hospitable to one another without grumbling;" (James 5:9 NKJV) "Do not grumble against one another, brethren, lest you be condemned;" (Philippians 2:14-16 NKJV) "Do all things without complaining and disputing that you may become blameless…and harmless, children of God without fault in the midst of a crooked and perverse generation, among whom you shine as lights in the world, holding fast the word of life…"

Our world is in need of nourishment - not just the nourishment of food, but the nourishment of "grace." When we are "dealing" with so much in our lives, why not deal out "the currency of grace" instead of grumbling? The fruits of the Spirit - the "Grace Currency"- consists of love, joy, peace, long-suffering, kindness, goodness, faithfulness, gentleness, self-control." (Gal. 5:22-23 ESV) May we choose to live as lights to the world which serve to shine to others the way of Christ.

Grumbling…Rumbling – "These are the things we can do without."
What the world needs is the "Currency of Grace." What's in your wallet?

Reflections

_____

_____

_____

_____

_____

_____

_____

_____

_____

_____

No More Power Outages

My husband built a house for our two outside dogs which he named "The Crystal Palace," not only because it was built specially for them, but also for its roof and side entry doors which were transparent – like glass. When we ventured out on the city streets after this latest winter incursion, the sight was breath-taking…crystalline – white-bright and shining – our neighborhood had also become a 'crystal palace'.

This diamond-studded show, however, soon took a back seat to a deeper, darker realization of damage, danger and despair. Broken and fallen trees (twisted as if in pain) and the subsequent damage to houses, vehicles and utility lines took one's breath in similar fashion as did one's initial response to the winter wonderland scene. I was amazed how it was that these two realities could co-exist but co-exist they did.

Both "beautiful and bruised" not only describes the winter landscape but is the consonant metaphor for our lives as believers in Christ. Saved as beautiful examples of His sacrifice on the cross, we also bear sin's scars as a consequence of willful or uninformed choices in our daily living on this earth. Like the shimmering but scarred winter landscape, we are diamonds in the rough, trusting in the power of the blood of Jesus to transform us to live in His "Crystal Palace" – Paradise. Would you be free from your burden of sin? There is wonder-working power in the precious blood of the Lamb.

In His Steps

Whether getting acclimated to wearing a new pair of glasses or just bundling-up in heavy winter garb, all of us need to manage our steps to prevent an accident. It is my lone responsibility to focus attention on the task at hand – which is to maintain balance and not fall.

I have fallen short implementing this strategy, however, regarding intentional strivings to purify my inner-self in my daily Christian walk. No matter how I try, I am unable to monitor myself with success. The more I focus on the barometer of self, the more my focus fades from the Lord and is riveted on the distortions of self and fear of missteps.

Our true life is made possible and comes into focus when we follow in the steps of Jesus. "In His Steps" there is no trip hazard. The way may be dangerous, but God is good. "There is no shadow of turning with Thee for Great is Thy faithfulness."

Draw us ever closer to You, blessed Savior, and set us on the straight path which always leads us home to Your Presence. In Jesus Name, we pray. Amen.

Being There

"Being there" for someone, anyone…even yourself, means being faithful. A movie released in the late 70's entitled <u>Being There</u> told the story of a simple-minded gardener who became the talk of the town by simply employing the wisdom he had gleaned from being a gardener for many years. This story made me reflect on the work our Heavenly Gardner employs as the Constant Gardner of our souls. He is rigidly but tenderly planting His seeds of love and wisdom in our hearts.

Ps.119:11 KJV admonishes: "Thy word have I hid in my heart, that I might not sin against Thee." This transformative miracle which yields fruit in its season, requires my simple faith and obedience to His Word so that the soil of my heart is prepared to receive the seeds placed there by the Creator.

"Being There" for others means to be faithful to love one another, but I cannot be there for others unless I make room for the plantings of the Constant Gardner in my heart that He made just for Himself. This is my constant prayer, and may it be yours as well, so that very truly, "all shall be well" with our souls and the souls we tend in God's Garden of Love.

Sing to the Lord a new song" (Ps. 96:1 NIV)

Many of us may have witnessed testimonial praise and worship music sung this week by believers in Ukraine and have longed to join them in a new song of praise to our God for hope and renewal…But what is a new song, unless it is the same song of "Hallelujah" sung with renewed expectation and commitment to answer the call of the love of God on our lives. God has always called me to Himself through music. Not surprising, I have been persuaded this week to bring three thoughts into focus. The first two thoughts are a favorite saying from an extremely powerful musician from my generation – the *love generation*…When the power of love overcomes the love of power the world will know peace (Jimi Hendrix.) Equally true is a saying from the African American evangelist, Sojourner Truth: "Truth is power and it prevails."

All turmoil in the world attests to competing so-called 'truths' proffered by person(s) who may not, in-truth, have the remotest idea of what "truth" really is. Holy scripture attests to the truth that defines all truth – Jesus said: "I am the Way, The Truth and the Life. No one comes to the Father except by Me." (John 14:6 NIV) The music of a subway choir in Ukraine or huddled masses in a shopping mall permeate and quicken our souls to become "one" with its message of peace. Let us commit ourselves to singing a 'new song'- a "Hallelujah" to renewed living of the "Truth" in the Love of Christ to this world, each and every waking moment, so that the world might awaken to the "Truth" that the "power of Love overcomes the "love of power" now and forever. Amen.

What time is it?
The acceptable time…Now

The word "now" means at the present moment of time. Our daily lives are absorbed in the here and now. But is there ever an instance when "now" does not mean right now? Dogs understand that when they are told to "Come" that it means right now - not later or when they feel like it. Why is it that humans don't get it? When instructed to respond in a proactive manner, a human will not necessarily choose to respond without delay unless the request is followed by "now!" Oddly enough, the operative words here are "choose" which denotes free will and "now" which is time sensitive.

Scripture clarifies the meaning of "now" as it concerns human relationships with a God Who has created us as reasoning beings. II Corinthians 6:2 answers the question, "What time is it? "For He (God) says: 'Behold, now is the acceptable time; behold, now is the day of salvation.' "God's Word uses "acceptable" to describe the welcoming character of "now" to choose to accept the divine gift of God's Spirit of Love in our lives to save us in the here and now and throughout eternity. Reason holds sway in the evidence for the critical nature of "now" found in Romans 8:1-2: "Therefore, there is "now" no condemnation for those who are in Christ Jesus, because through Christ Jesus the law of the Spirit who gives life has set you free from the law of sin and death." Moreover, God is not bound by time as we know it - the "now" path for our journey of hope has been and is established as proclaimed in Ephesians 5:8: "For you were once darkness, but now you are light in the Lord. Live as children of light."

"Because" was the last song ever written by The Beatles (Abbey Road album 1969). It spoke of eternity in the here and now with these lyrics: "Love is old, Love is new; Love is all, Love is you." As a believer in Christ, it is natural for me to capitalize the "y" making you into "You" referring to the Eternal Lord of Love. It is my belief that, all those held "now" and forever in the arms of the Savior because of His saving Grace would agree with the following amendment to the lyrics previously quoted:

"Love is old, Love is new…Love is vow, Love is now."

What time is it!　　　It is always now!　　　Let us live as "children of light."

Reflections

_____

_____

_____

_____

_____

_____

Reflections

Season of Lent

Surrender
by Lana Lee Marler

There is a point beneath the wake
When all the senses blur;
Where sight and sound and life's dull ache
Sink past all things that were.

Pressing desires and thoughts grown still
As once upon a dream,
Drift now so gently on the will
Of the Maker of the stream.

What grand design has brought me thus,
So, poised in space and time?
With outstretched arms as on a cross,
My life will soon be Thine.

O God, my heart cries out to You.
Leave not my soul in death;
But raise me up to life anew,
Filled with Your holy breath.

https://heavens.jacobsladdercdc.org/home/surrender

Treading deep water?
Seek the meek connection

As a kid, my experiences with water, other than the bathtub, were limited to our local Y.M.C.A. where my aunt gave swimming lessons. As the oldest child in our family, I must say I did not set a good example for my siblings, especially when the water was over my head. Panicked to this day, I avoid the deep end of the pool, even though the skill of treading water was added to my pool toolbox under my aunt's tutelage. The notion of being "in over one's head" in different circumstances is familiar. Whether bad relationship, career, health or a series of poor decisions, all of us have felt the "no way out" feeling of panic and yelled in our spirits "somebody help me!"

In 1970, Diana Ross released a song for her generation (or any generation, for that matter) with applicable lyrics as follows:
"Reach out and touch somebody's hand, Make this world a better place, if you can…Just try." In my opinion, this is the signature song for meekness, i.e., humble and gentle as expressed in the mindset of scripture. Human society more often harbors the notion of being meek as weak, non-violent, submissive and going with the flow instead of making a stand. But according to scripture, being meek is not less, it is more. There resides in a meek person great power, however, that power is under control. The power of meekness is having humility toward God and toward others, in that, a meek person does not use power over others to benefit oneself. The apostle Paul urges "to live a life worthy of the calling [we] have received. Be completely humble and gentle; be patient, bearing with one another in love" (Ephesians 4:1-2).

That is why, "when the storms of life are raging," the meek person does not think of himself first but instead is drawn to extend a helping hand to others as did Jesus, (Who) "being in very nature God, did not consider equality with God something to be used to his own advantage; rather, he made himself nothing by taking the very nature of a servant, being made in human likeness. And being found in appearance as a man, he humbled himself by becoming obedient to death—even death on a cross!" (Philippians 2:6-8) In submission to His Father, Jesus offered everything - His hands extended in daily life to help others and then extended and nailed to a cross by the power of submissive love.

It is an indelible image I still hold of my aunt's hand extended to me as I struggled to tread in deep water. When you find yourself or others in similar circumstance of finding the way through deep water, "just try" to seek the meek connection: "Reach out and touch somebody's hand…and make this world a better place, if you can…Just try" with God's help.

Reflections

Reflections

_____

_____

_____

_____

_____

_____

_____

_____

_____

_____

_____

_____

_____

_____

_____

_____

_____

Broken Record or Not...

In the wake of this past Ash Wednesday which began the Season of Lent, my remembrance of the imposition of ashes on my forehead in the shape of a cross accompanied by the words: "Remember that you are dust and to dust you shall return" keeps playing in my head like a broken record on an old phonograph.
All human beings are broken and in need of more than mending...the state of the soul requires that it be made "new" by the power of blood of Jesus shed for the sins of the world. But the pit of despair which awaits those persons prone to introspection is that of condemnation of self.

How can this be the reality of a believer in Christ when all we need to do is embrace God's love and forgiveness for all our sins...whether they be committed willfully, in ignorance or just force of habit. A line from a gospel music favorite asks: "Would you be free from your burden of sin?" The answer is: Of course, we want to be free from the burden of sin which so easily besets us. The Lord God has already provided everything needed to free ourselves from the burden of sin. However, we must be participants in the process through the purging of focusing on self. The soul's daily requirement is a fresh unraveling of unrighteousness so that its twisted fragments are left behind and we proceed in faith on the path forward prepared by our Lord in the promise of scripture: "A voice of one calling in the desert, 'Prepare the way for the Lord, make straight paths for Him. Every valley shall be filled in, every mountain and hill made low. The crooked roads shall become straight, the rough ways smooth. And all mankind will see God's salvation'" (Luke 3:5,6 NIV)

Therefore, it is a welcome and needful labor of the soul to cast aside self-recrimination and instead wholly embrace that we are forever made new before God through the sacrifice of Jesus. In His great love, He has made the crooked places straight in our soul's daily strivings, in the remembrances of deeds past, and He is leveling the mountain paths of the future…

In this penitential Season of Lent, I am comforted by God's promises while I am reminded to repent and believe the gospel (Mark 1:15 KJV), so that the shattered fragments of my song here on earth will at last come to finer melody in the Presence of God.

Reflections

_____

_____

_____

_____

_____

_____

_____

_____

The Nature of Grace

Most of us say "Grace" before we partake a meal. To many people, it may still be just a custom with not much thought of what we say i.e.., "For that which we are about to receive make us truly grateful." Do we really think about what we're saying when we are saying it? Are we indeed truly grateful or do we just think having a meal is something that we have in due course each day without reminding ourselves that there are others in the world who are not so fortunate?

There are other graces for which we offer daily thanks. One note of grace in my life (and not a lesser grace to be sure) is that we enjoy sharing our home with two dogs who live outside - one is elderly and the other is a 1-1/2 year-old rescue dog we took in a few months ago. Both are sweet members of our household. Our elderly dog (Buddy) is a gentle male, sweet-spirited and not pushy, always waiting his turn. His new younger sibling, however, was on the street her whole life - having to fight, scrounge, and hunt for whatever she could get to survive. In God's providence, we named our new rescue dog, Gracie. Gracie has sweet ways too, but is opposite in nature, in that she is going to push to get her due. In her experience and perhaps it is her nature as well, she thinks if she doesn't push and grab, then she might not make it to see another meal. We welcome Gracie into our lives as a gift by way of the grace of God.

God's relationship of grace with humanity is not dissimilar. His grace giftings are on the just and the unjust. The nature of Grace is resilient and tough...Grace does the easy things and Grace does the hard things, as well. I am reminded of a song released in 1968 by Three Dog Night called "Easy To Be Hard". The lyrics ask and answer: "How can people be so heartless? How can people be so cruel? Easy to be hard; Easy to say, "No." As its hallmark, Conservatism and the Conservative tradition of Christianity would say: "There is one right answer to every question." It's easy to be hard and equally, sometimes it's hard to be easy when it comes to forgiveness. The call of grace is answered by Christ to forgive seventy times seven. What does that mean? Nobody counts how many times they forgive another. The Lord was saying to be generous and keep forgiving but he did not say forgive forever - end of discussion. Acts 17:30 NIV makes this proclamation: "In the past, God overlooked such ignorance, but now he commands all people everywhere to repent. "Forgiving seventy times seven means that at some point we draw the line and embrace another truth - the equation must change, otherwise the truth of the what the other person needs to be aware of and grow into will not be communicated. They will continue their behavior until someone at the right time, in the right place, and the right way says out of love: "OK, we're not gonna do things like this anymore."

"It's easy to be hard" and "It's hard to be easy" is the nature and truth of "tough love". Tough love is what we are all called to practice as followers of Christ. He healed the sick and fed the multitudes, but he also cleansed the temple and hung on the cross for our transgressions. Tough love is Grace, and the nature of Grace is Love, though at times, it is tough to give and receive. It's hard to be easy and easy to be hard. Thanks be to God that His nature is *Grace*.

Everything is relative…Or is it?

Relative about what and to whom? We've all heard the saying that one man's food is another man's poison. Be it love, hate, life, death, sorrow or joy - the topics matter to each individual person, relative to themselves. Even the selection of the topics are relative issues. If that is the case, then it would seem relevant to invest our lives in the things that have lasting value - eternal value, that is, the Truth of God, the Creator of all things. However, the issue remains: every person decides how to invest the treasure of self - being drawn rightly or not to a certain way of life. It is "smoke and mirrors" offered by tricksters in this earthly existence, intended to make you believe that something is being done or is true, when it is not.

A "relevant" story from scripture can be found in Acts 16:22-34 KJV. Community leaders (inspired to protect and revenge their own wallets) incite a crowd which results in the wrongful flogging and imprisonment of Paul and Silas. For many, being stripped, beaten and shackled in a prison cell represents the "poison" of what the "smoke and mirrors" food in life has to offer. In this story, the contrary is found wafting up from the damp and dark recesses of their cell. Hymns were being sung to God, no less - birthed from the truth of God's calling and revelation in the lives of Paul and Silas and in testimony to their jailer and cellmates.

The "smoke and mirrors" of the tricksters did not obscure and veil the truth for these disciples of Christ but rather revealed the transforming Presence of God. As the pillar cloud led the Children of Israel in the desert, so the "smoke" is relevant to the Divine. Likewise, the "mirrors" reflect God's image (compared to our own sinful reflections) into the spirit of man, thereby drawing humanity to salvation and transformation.

As followers of Christ, we've a story to tell to the nations: "Sing to the Lord; praise his name. Each day proclaim the good news that He saves." (Ps. 96 CSB) Like Paul and Silas, let us sing praises to God in the 'relative' darkness of our lives and adopt the "whistle while you work" lifestyle, as we tell the story of salvation to the nations of the world by the living of our lives in joy and relevance to the Truth of Christ, our Lord and Savior.

Reflections

_____

_____

_____

_____

_____

_____

_____

_____

_____

_____

In and Out of Season

The polite emergence of the blessings of Spring is demanding attention these days. Blooming trees, and yellow buttercups grace the landscapes of our communities. They are the fragile but concrete evidence of the hope of Spring. But are they indeed fragile? Their very existence belies that truth…they are in fact, "War Flowers." They share themselves in testimony with delicate heads raised, having thrived, despite the cruel pangs of winter's cold bombardments.

We as Christians can relate to the lives of the "War Flowers" who battle and contend with the elements, be they good or ill, so that their 'Hope of Spring' is realized. I Peter 3:15 ESV admonishes: "…in your hearts honor Christ the Lord as holy, always being prepared to make a defense to anyone who asks you for a reason for the hope that is in you; yet do it with gentleness and respect."

It is with gentleness and respect that the flowers surprise the surface of the earth in witness to the victory of the hope of new life that calls them to rise. In no less fashion, the believer, in-dwelled by the Spirit of God, has Christ's love and posture of tender persuasion to share the reason for hope of new life and resurrection. It is in Christ that our hope springs eternal because He is eternal. His promises are sure 'in and out of season' because the battle is already won on our behalf.

Let us rejoice and bloom like "War Flowers," whose very nature it is to bear witness to the hope that is in them. The call of God on Nature is one of consistent preparation. Likewise, His call on the nature of the believer in Christ is constant (in and out of season) to always be prepared to witness to that hope. In so doing, that hope can spring eternal in the hearts of any and all seekers of new life. In layman's language…"If you stay ready, you won't have to get ready." Amen.

Reflections

_____

_____

_____

_____

_____

_____

_____

_____

_____

_____

_____

Holy Week

Palm Sunday

Palms Up

We rehearse the Triumphal Entry of Jesus into Jerusalem in our worship settings on Palm Sunday (the first day of Holy Week), with the waving of palm branches accompanied by shouts of praise and exaltation to the King of Israel. Having been raised in a conservative Baptist environment, I was not accustomed to the raising of open-palmed hands in praise in church services. As I grew into an adult, however, I had more opportunities for worship where this practice was the norm. I am so grateful to say now that hands raised in praise are a form of worshipful expression which blesses me to this day.

The journey during Holy Week begins on this high note but if we are being honest, all of us would admit that in our church services "there are only sinners in the room." In the words of Dennis the Menace (you know the comic strip) we share his sentiments and find ourselves likewise out of sorts: "I'm just sittin' around feeling guilty...how about you?" It's been a long day and I behaved for most of it...That's got to count for something" or "Anyway, rules shouldn't be so easy to break." Sound familiar? Excuses...excuses, i.e.., "the devil made me do it" is how we explain away our sinful behavior.

The Gospels recount that when we reach the end of Holy Week, many unholy acts have been perpetrated on the Son of Man by "sinners such as I". The suffering Jesus uttered these words: "It is finished" (John 19:30 ESV); "Into Thy hands I commend my spirit" (Luke 23:46 KJV), as He surrendered His life and died on behalf of those He came to save.

One of the two thieves crucified with Jesus reviled Him as an imposter and powerless to save Himself or anyone else. However, the second condemned criminal is penitent and believes then and there in the saving grace of God…he requests that the Savior remember him when He comes into His kingdom. All that he is and has done in his life, he surrenders in faith. His faith is rewarded…In the words of Christ, "Today, thou shalt be with me in Paradise." (Luke 23:43)

So here too, during this "Holiest" of weeks, may we experience the journey from praise to penitence. With the thief on the cross, who died in faith and surrender to the saving grace of God, let us be open-palmed, reaching upward to heaven and proclaiming: "All to Jesus, I surrender; "I Surrender All."

Palms Up, Everyone!

The Deposition of Compassion by Daniel Bonnell
Good Friday

The Beauty of Your Love
by Lana Lee Marler

O Lamb of God, the beauty of Your Love;
Flows through all time and space from above.
But, all the while, my soul knew not its name;
'Til I beheld Your Cross of sin and shame.

O Christ, my Savior, seems as if I see;
A thorny crown, Your head weighed down.
How can this be, such perfect love for me;
Bore all my guilt by hanging on a tree.

O Lamb of God, Love shines from heaven's shore;
My risen Lord, alive forevermore.
No tomb can hold - "O Death, where is thy sting?"
Throughout the ages, I will ever sing -

What wondrous Love is this, O my soul!

https://heavens.jacobsladdercdc.org/home/beauty

50

Reflections

Everywhere I go I feel love…

In these past weeks, during what some may refer to as "The Latter Days" because of the upheaval in the world, I have had a common and unsettling occurrence of unexplained weeping. When I shared this with my sister, she commented that she was experiencing this same tendency to weep. I was comforted when I remembered my mentor in the Faith used to say: "Tears are a sign of the Presence of the Spirit." The deep well in my soul from which the tears swell and overflow outward affirm the words of scripture: "Deep calleth unto deep." Ps. 42:7 KJV

As a child I learned a song which you may be familiar with as well. You might also remember we used outward hand movements to express the inner truth of the song while we sang: "Deep and wide; Deep and wide; There's a fountain flowing, deep and wide." Its' message is as clear as the Fountain of God it describes - a fountain of mercy which is ever-flowing to address the sinful needs of the human soul.

No song is born in a vacuum, least of all the "Deep and Wide" song. It requires "context" - that is, cavernous depths filled to overflowing (concave to convex) from which meaning is derived - hence, a love song is established. The depth of human need draws the unfathomable resources from God, just as God's mercy will not be denied in its outpouring of God's Goodness to fill that depth of need.

Psalm 91:14-16 GNT attests to the "Love" contract all believers in Christ enjoy with our Father God, who says: "I will save those who love me and will protect those who acknowledge me as Lord. When they call to me, I will answer them; when they are in trouble, I will be with them. I will rescue them and honor them. I will reward them with long life; I will save them."

The Presence of the Holy Spirit of God goes behind and before us and holds us everywhere we are, comforting and steadying us in the trials of our lives. It is no wonder that "everywhere I go I feel love" …so much so, that God's holding me, squeezes out my tears in testament to the joy and comfort of His love and presence. "Blessed Assurance, Jesus Is Mine. This is my story; This is my song" …Not born in a vacuum but in the context of Christ's blood poured-out for the depth of my need…This is my love song. May it be yours as well.

Reflections

Hope in the Heights

We had a humble but profound visitation at our house on Easter weekend. It wasn't kinfolk barnstorming our door or a rarely tasted succulent Easter feast. Rather, it was a surprise visit from a previously undisclosed neighboring bird - an albino sparrow - white as snow and equipped with an untold ability to bless us in its vista. We had never heard of an albino sparrow nor fathomed one possible to appear unannounced in our back yard. I thought the Easter Season of Resurrection to be such an appropriate time to receive this revelation. White is the signature color of the Season. We wear white robes, adorn our churches in white linens, white Easter lilies and we rejoice in the revelation of light, new life and hope. It is a real and tangible hope which is untainted, because as believers in Christ and His Resurrection from the dead, Christ resides in our hearts…He is our hope for life beyond death.

Even as a child, I remember a beloved song about the struggle of hope in life. It was a song by Frank Sinatra called "High Hopes" about an ant trying to move a rubber tree plant…He had to have "high hopes; high apple pie in the sky hopes" in order to complete his task. On a similar vein, another song comes to mind which you may have heard as a teenager called "Hold on, I'm Comin'". A song by Sam and Dave from 1966, it is also a human testament about hope in life. These musical metaphors of hope were born from the ordinary, but they represent the extraordinary. We have hope because the Lord says He is with us to help us to endure in all our struggles and He is coming for us to take us to heaven - "high apple pie in the sky hope."

Holy scripture affirms that God made all human beings in His image. In the light of that gift of life, we have the heritage of hope from our Creator. All of us however, are well aware of those times when our hope fades. But how can that be? How can hope fade when it is resident in us? How can we lose hope when the hope of glory is part of us in Christ's indwelling Spirit? It doesn't mean that when there is a loss and we grieve (as the disciples grieved when they lost their Lord on good Friday) that we don't cry, but we have the hope now that the disciples did not have then before Jesus' resurrection. Yet we can still lie in our beds, as I have done most recently, and fill my ears with tears over loss and regret. Grieving doesn't erase the fact that there is hope - real, supernatural hope, born of the Spirit of Christ that lives in me.

As scripture says in I John 3:3 ESV: "And everyone who thus hopes in Him purifies himself as He is pure." Hope is the filter of life - refining and removing impurities (hence, the pristine white Easter adornments) so that all that we do and say and think and work for is purified by the resident hope in our bodies. "His Eye is on the Sparrow" … even the creation and revelation of a white sparrow instills us with hope and quickens our spirits; "High Hopes" to finish our task; "High in the Sky Hopes" to reach our heavenly home at last; "Hold on, He's Coming" Amen!

For This Reason

To they who have come out of the great ordeal…On the special Sunday designated to honor and esteem our mothers, I am reminded of a song released in 2021 by Mac Powell, "Love is the Reason." It begins with a mother's response to her child asking why go to church when the service is long and boring. Her answer simply put: "Love is the reason that I go." In this context the great ordeal (just referenced) is pregnancy and childbirth and then subsequently, the mother giving her life to raise her child in love. Love is the gig…It is a hard gig but not without its share of joys and blessings. Revelation 7 (NRSVA), also refers to the great ordeal which is substantive as John relates a portion of his post-apocalyptic vision: "All the angels were standing around the throne and around the elders and the four living creatures, and they fell on their faces before the throne and worshiped God…Then one of the elders addressed me, saying, 'Who are these, robed in white, and where have they come from?' I said to him, 'Sir, you are the one that knows.' Then he said to me, 'These are they who have come out of the great ordeal; they have washed their robes and made them white in the blood of the Lamb. *For this reason,* they are before the throne of God, and worship Him day and night within his temple, and the One Who is seated on the throne will shelter them…for the Lamb at the center of the throne will be their Shepherd."

So, "Love" is the reason now and always, whereby sacrifice is requisite to life - human life and eternal life. Thanks be to God for the gift of the love of mothers and the love of our Savior Who gave them to us and exemplified true sacrificial living and loving for all mankind. "Love" is the reason the Son of Man came to give His life as a ransom for many… ***For This Reason.***

Reflections

"That'll Be the Day"

There's a famous saying: "My heroes have always been cowboys." Though the statement is well-known, it makes it no less true for me in my life. The movies and television shows in my childhood were rife with variations on the theme known as "The Cowboy Way." My own father was known to the family as "Our Duke" after John Wayne, the iconic cowboy. Even my own husband had a nickname in high school, "Cowboy Bill."

Apart from the skills, strength and bravado of the typical cowboy, the primary attraction to the masses was the code of ethics which the cowboy adhered to: 1. Speak the truth; 2. Do the right thing and 3. Respect others. The tenets of "The Cowboy Way" offered a standard to live by which engendered a feeling of balanced comfort and safety, very familiar to the scriptural lessons we were taught in Sunday School. So, "That'll be the day" (from John Wayne in the classic western movie, The Searchers) when "The Cowboy Way" is transformed into "The Way of Christ" … the way of living and speaking the truth in love, which is paramount for those who bear His name - Christians. In Ephesians 4:15 NIV scripture states: "Speaking the truth in love, we will grow to become in every respect the mature body of Him Who is the head, that is, Christ."

Always speaking the truth is one thing but speaking the truth in love is something else. Speaking the truth, can and is often used by many as a "rod" to reprimand, berate or punish. In the twenty-first chapter of the Gospel of John, Jesus relates His version of telling the truth in love - a cautionary tale in which the three denials by Peter before the crucifixion are responded to by Christ in a restorative fashion i.e., telling the truth in love. Jesus addresses Peter's three instances of betrayal with three questions designed to remind him of the love he seemingly had forsaken. Moreover, the question-and-answer narrative provides Peter with the opportunity to respond in affirmation to that love and then a way forward to demonstrate it. "Do you love Me? Feed My sheep." (John 21:15-17 KJV)

Our Lord and Savior came into this world to be the mediator between God and man - the perfect balance between He Who knew no sin and the sinner He was sent to redeem. More than "The Cowboy Way" mentioned earlier, Jesus offers in this scripture passage "The Jesus Way" of not only telling the truth but telling the truth in love. Thus, forgiveness and restoration of relationship is offered as He wraps Peter in the loving embrace of His teaching. Thanks be to God that "speaking the truth in love, we will grow to become in every respect the mature body of Him Who is the head, that is, Christ."

So, "That'll be the day when you say good-bye" to the former code which is not uniformly tinctured with compassion (please forgive, but I couldn't resist the Buddy Holly line.) It is time to "saddle up" and in so doing, let us all strive to bring the church up to "code" by adhering to the Code of Ethics of the Kingdom of Christ which is Love "What a Day That Will Be" when my Jesus I shall see and He says, "Well done, my good and faithful servant."

Bumps in the Road?...Get a Grip!

Except for the occasional stay in a motel, my husband and I travel in a plain white cargo van he customized for us to live in on the road. We are blessed to enjoy its comfort, but the ride is not devoid of shakes, rattles and squeaks. Because of the interior additions, i.e., bed, cabinets, closet, sink, shelving, etc., it is my opinion that they account for the occasional auditory disturbances as we travel. It has become an ongoing debate centered around whether any noise problem is inherent to the van or just attributable to the bumpy road. On a recent trip out West, we confronted the ultimate challenge to our van on the Shafer Trail in Utah. Ignoring the warning sign that only all-terrain four-wheel drive vehicles could traverse the trail, we pushed forward between non-stop bumping and the dodging of low-hanging rocks as the trail shook the van and our souls to its foundations. Through prayer and thanksgiving to God for his provision and protection, we resumed our journey in hope on the road unforeseen ahead.

The disciples of Christ had experienced a far worse shaking of their foundations in the experiences surrounding the crucifixion, death and what seemed like a mysterious (and in need of confirmation) resurrection from the grave by their Teacher and Rabbi. The walk on the road to Emmaus provided the disciples with the opportunity to once again experience Christ's presence in their lives, to gain new insight into the powerful grace of God and thereby renew and form relationships in the faith as a foundation for the maturity needed to answer the call of discipleship on their lives.

Luke 24:13-31 KJV (In Summary)

Two disciples, walking the road to Emmaus, were in conversation about everything that had happened concerning Jesus of Nazareth. Jesus appeared on the road and walked with them, but they were prevented from recognizing him. When Jesus asked what they were talking about, they were in disbelief that he was unaware of what had happened to the prophet Jesus...his trial, execution and death. Moreover, Jesus' body was reported missing by bystanders, and some had witnessed seeing angels at the empty tomb. Jesus remarked that they were slow to believe and then he explained to them what was said in all the Scriptures concerning the Messiah. Rather than continuing his journey, Jesus was persuaded to stay with the disciples and sat at table with them. He broke bread and gave it to them, whereupon their eyes were opened, and they knew who he was before he disappeared from their sight.

Having shared the broken bread received from the hand of the resurrected Jesus, the disciples become "one" in purpose and proceed hand-in-hand down the road of faith. The road is not without its obstacles and bumps, so that a sudden jolt requires strengthening of grip and resolve. To journey in faith means they are assured because they walk on the "soft pavement of prayer." For it is prayer and praise which always lead to hope and healing on the road to glory. Thanks be to God. Amen.

The Rapture of Rupture

The word "rapture" is taken from the Latin "rapio" which means to be caught up or taken away. (I Thessalonians 4:13-18 ASV) Just recently, I heard someone say that a person cannot believe in heaven and then be sad when someone they love goes there - whether via death or the forthcoming rapture of the church. Although the actual word "rapture" is not mentioned in the Bible, scriptural teachings concerning Jesus' return to call His own unto Himself, both living and dead, to meet Him in the air at the end of the age, held major significance in the church where I was raised. So much so, that as kids, my younger sisters and I used to speculate how we would feel being lifted up into the air at the rapture. I remember one of my sisters purposed to keep her legs straight and together while being taken away in that ascension of believers - a very real event in which we invested even our child-like faith. As children, we had no real notion of death, but the powerful hope of the rapture was born in our spirits even as a "rapturous" joy.

If being caught up in "rapture" is universal and real in emotion and experience, then it would not be inaccurate to apply the label of "rupture" (to breach, disturb or part by violence) as its counterpart in human existence. The fabric of life is certainly in a state of rupture when it is threatened by death. It's not a stretch to attribute to most human beings the desire that right up until the very last moment, by some miracle they will cheat death…that is, to beat the odds and avoid death even when it seems an impossibility.

After a visionary encounter with Christ, the Apostle Paul was later imprisoned in Rome and wrote a letter to the church in Philippi in which he expressed a very different opinion on the notion of "cheating death" Paul writes in Philippians 1:21-25 (CEV) "If I live, it will be for Christ, and if I die, I will gain even more. I don't know what to choose. I could keep on living and doing something useful. It is a hard choice to make. I want to die and be with Christ, because this would be much better. But I know that all of you still need me. This is why I am sure I will stay on to help you grow and be happy in your faith."

St. Paul's own words testify to being torn between two desires - For Paul to die is gain because it is better by far to be with Christ but to live for St. Paul is gain as well, because for him, to live *is* Christ - "If I live on in the flesh, this will mean fruit from my labor." At this point in his life, for St. Paul to cheat death would also mean to cheat life, i.e.., the call on his life to be a servant leader to build up the church. This calling, however, includes hardship, persecution and suffering, but would also be fruitful in love and service, always in the hope of God's glory being manifested by the presence of the Holy Spirit.

What are some ways that we as believers in Christ cheat life in our efforts to cheat death? 1)We avoid the difficult situations we are confronted with in the service of humanity and the life of the church; 2) We trust the counsel of others instead of trusting God's Word and the leading of His Holy Spirit; 3) We indulge our own desires for affirmation and not purpose to live in humility as Christ did by giving His life in love for humanity. It is because He died for all and now lives in resurrected glory that we are called and able to live and serve His Kingdom here on earth or in heaven. The choice is ours as it was for Christ and the Apostle Paul…to choose the "rapture of rupture" and die to self that others may live. Praise be to Christ! Amen.

Reflections

_____

_____

_____

_____

_____

_____

_____

_____

_____

_____

_____

_____

_____

_____

_____

_____

_____

Pentecost

O Breath of Life by Bessie Porter Head
Adapted Lyrics and Music by Lana Lee Marler

O Breath of Life, come sweeping through us,
Revive your world with life and power.
O Breath of Life, come, cleanse, renew us,
And fit your people to meet this hour.

O Wind of Life, come, bend us, break us,
Till humbly we confess our need.
Then in your tenderness remake us,
Revive, restore, for this we plead.

O Breath of Life, come sweeping through us,
Revive your world with life and power.
O Breath of Life, come, cleanse, renew us,
And fit your people to meet this hour.

O Breath of Love, come, live within us,
Renewing thought and will and heart.
Creator of all, come afresh to win us,
Revive your world in every part.

https://heavens.jacobsladdercdc.org/home/breath

Reflections

Ordinary Time
Season after Pentecost

Back to the Garden
by Lana Lee Marler

I long to see myself in a knowing sky;
And be wrapped in warm colors as down I lie,
Then closing my eyes, find rest in the beauty
Of the Love song that has ever called to me.

O sing me to sleep and sing me awake,
And sing me alive because my soul aches
To give my whole self to the Music within
Calling me back to the Garden again.

There are holes in my soul that trouble me.
Holes blocking out light and then letting none leave;
Darkening portals of loathing and fear,
These holes through which I cannot see or hear.

My soul's dark cradle is stirred in the night.
By shimmering echoes of belonging and light;
Summoning yearnings for deep harmony
With all things present or coming to be.

O sing me to sleep and sing me awake,
And sing me alive because my soul aches
To give my whole self to the Music within
Calling me back to the Garden again.

The Garden of Peace whereby Love was first held;
The Garden of Peace where Love holds me still.

https://heavens.jacobsladdercdc.org/home/garden

Sealed with a Kiss

One would be correct to assume that children and their parents have consumed my prayerful attention once again this week. The goodnight kiss from parents to their children holds such life-long significance - afterwards, the parent dims the light and leaves the room, making the way gently and quietly down a dark hallway. To the child it seems an interminable length of time before the shadows of night fade and the loneliness of slumber's separation is supplanted by the comfort of reunion in the light of day. As a child, I experienced the good night kiss as securing my station…both approved and beloved; securing my status as safe, being situated alone in a darkened bedroom; and securing my faith and hope that all shall be well.

The kiss is a tool of humanity used in a variety of settings to denote affection, approval, respect, acquiescence/submission or even betrayal as was the case in the gospel accounts of Judas' kiss of Christ in the Garden of Gethsemane. "You may kiss the bride" are the final words a minister utters at the conclusion of a marriage ceremony which signifies to onlookers that the deal is sealed…" sealed with a kiss."

Using the above referenced axiom virtually compels me to think of the song by its name "Sealed with a Kiss, written in 1960 by Peter Udell and Gary Geld and later recorded by Bobby Vinton. The song lyrics are pertinent to the theme and dynamics of Pentecost as they refer to a love relationship having to endure the grief of temporary physical separation - the affirmation of that love commitment is sent in a missive which is "sealed with a kiss." The Holy Spirit (The Comforter) was given to the children of God at Pentecost to "seal the deal." We read in the book of Acts 2:1-4 NIV: "When the day of Pentecost came, they (the disciples) were all together in one place. Suddenly a sound like the blowing of a violent wind came from heaven and filled the whole house where they were sitting. They saw what seemed to be tongues of fire that separated and came to rest on each of them. All of them were filled with the Holy Spirit and began to speak in other tongues as the Spirit enabled them."

The gift of the Holy Spirit "seals the deal" and seals us with God's loving kiss of Presence for eternity. The Comforter descending upon those waiting in faith and His Presence resting on each as a tongue of fire, is testimony to the outpouring missive of God, i.e.., His love letter taking residence in the heart of the believer in Christ the Savior, Who had just recently ascended to the glory of heaven. At Pentecost, God as the parent gave His children the ability to speak and understand His Voice in other languages as The Spirit gave them utterance. As a child of God, we can call out in the night of our situation, down the darkened, quiet hallway of our souls and know we speak the language of God which He will always hear and answer. The Day of Pentecost is a declaration that as children of Almighty God, we will never have to be alone in the dark again. Praise His Name forever!

Let It Rain…

A heat wave has descended on our state. With the prospect of rain not in the near forecast, drought conditions prevail. Cautionary tales abound regarding the risks of this unprovoked situation. But unfortunately, control switches for the weather do not exist like in a futuristic movie! All must deal with this circumstance as best they can. The ovens of our hearts do not have off buttons either…they are always in use - baking, broiling, warming or white hot - depending on the entrees our spirits have concocted and placed inside.

The mercy of rain is the remedy - *Downpour* to answer *Drought*! A song released by Jesus Culture in 2010 prayerfully beseeches that the floodgates of heaven open to "let it rain" down the mercies of heaven. One such account of the mercies of heaven raining down to "sweep the weep" broiling in the oven of despair, can be found in Luke 8:26-39 CEV. Jesus in His compassion to an unprovoked human calamity, heals a man possessed by demons and then mercifully permits the demons to enter a herd of swine instead of being eternally cast into the Abyss. Needless to say, the man delivered from the attack of legions of inner demons was profuse in his gratitude to Jesus. However, the neighbors of the possessed man were dismayed and filled with fear - After all, they had just witnessed their pig livelihood stampede down a mountainside to their deaths.

Was this a demonstration of the age of the Aquarius - the Water Bearer of mercies raining down **or** the age of Nefarious - as evidenced by the fear-filled responses of those nay-sayers more concerned with themselves than the miraculous "rain" of mercy and peace on a suffering soul. What is cooking in the kitchen of your heart today? Faith? Fear? Gratitude? Maditude? Let the

Sunshine in, so that the heat in your heart's oven can be that of love, mercy, forgiveness and grace. Or in other words... "Let It Rain".

Reflections

_____

_____

_____

_____

_____

_____

_____

_____

_____

_____

_____

_____

_____

_____

What the World Needs Now…

It does not surprise me, as I reflected on this past week, that a song kept resurfacing in my heart. It was written in 1926 by Grace W. Owens, *O Who Can Make a Flower*? The voices of children singing it from my youth keep echoing in my head…

"O Who can make a flower?
I'm sure I can't, can you?
O Who can make a flower?
No one but God 'tis true. "

Hopefully, you were blessed to hear and sing this song (and similar songs of innocent praise to God) as a child.   But "always and in all times", there have been children all over the world not able to join in the chorus due to suffering, not because their hearts were tarnished, but because their innocence was robbed by a tarnished world. Robb Elementary School in Texas was "robbed" this past week… Children's innocent voices were stolen - silenced in this life but not the next…" of such is the kingdom of heaven." (Matt. 19:14 KJV) There was no way out of a locked room, when a "no child *left behind* attitude" of the shooter ended in slaughter. The children have blood on their faces from being shot in the head but all of us have blood on our hands, in that we are responsible for the sinfulness of a world that would allow this unprovoked carnage. However, we are promised in scripture that God's mercies are new every morning (it could be spelled *mourning* in this instance) In Lamentations 3:21-23 KJV, Jeremiah wrote a testament to hope and love: "This I recall to my mind, therefore have, I hope. It is of the Lord's mercies that we are not consumed, because his compassions fail not. They are new every morning: "great is thy faithfulness."

What is the answer to the question we don't even know how to ask…How do we mourn such a loss? Jacob Knapp in 1845 answered this question in his song, *Give me Jesus* - It begins thus: *And I heard the mourner say, And I heard the mourner say, And I heard the mourner say, Give me Jesus. Give me Jesus; Give me Jesus; You may have all the world, Give me Jesus.*

Holy Father, forgive us when we place the ways of this world before Your ways. Thank You for giving us, Jesus, the sinless Lamb of God, who shed His blood and gave His life to pay the sin debt of all who have rebelled against Your Word and Your ways. What the world needs now is Love - *always and in all ways.* Teach us to learn to love and live in Your Love. For it is in the name of Jesus we pray. Amen.

Whatsoever…

You may or may not have experienced what is called an "earworm" or "brainworm" - a syndrome which relies on brain networks that are involved in perception, emotion, memory and spontaneous thought. It sounds gross but actually it is a catchy and/or memorable piece of music or saying that continuously occupies a person's mind even after it is no longer being played or spoken about.

As a musician, this particular phenomena, for better or worse, plagues me a lot. This past week we went to see the newly released film, <u>Top Gun Maverick</u> at the theater (sequel to 1986 movie about U.S. Navy fighter pilot training) and then proceeded to watch the <u>Top Gun</u> original on Prime Video. It was the theme song "Danger Zone" recorded by Kenny Loggins that has played over and over in my mind as a consequence. And a "Danger Zone" it is, when a thought, memory, fear or something as simple as random song lyrics and melody consumes us to the point of control - a feeling of "No Exit".

While on vacation the first of this month, we visited a friend in Louisa, Virginia who has been called to a ministry of worship enlightenment relating to prayer, music, Christian community and the peace of God. The time we spent at "The Community of Peace", sharing in worship together, renewed commitment to allowing our time with the Lord to be devoid of distraction, that is, open-ended freedom in the flow of experiencing God as the Holy Spirit leads. My friend described the dynamic of removing focus from a disruptive thought or image as letting go of a cloud - To hold a cloud in one's hand is not possible in the first place, so it makes little sense to foster the illusion of its control.

Philippians 4:8 KJV admonishes how best to honor the path of the Spirit: "Finally, brethren, whatsoever things are true, whatsoever things are honest, whatsoever things are just, whatsoever things are pure, whatsoever things are lovely, whatsoever things are of good report; if there be any virtue, and if there be any praise, think on these things."

As human beings, danger, struggle and sacrifice go hand in hand but **there is freedom from the "No Exit" experiences in our daily lives**, whether it is in chasing or being chased by a certain thought, memory or emotion during the day or even in the still of the night on our beds…It is the strength and freedom of choice in the Spirit of God. And what is the Sound of Freedom? When it first presents, the sound of freedom is not a piece of music, as one might guess from this topic of discussion, but it is the sound of metal clanging against metal…as the nails are driven into the hands and feet of the Savior as He gave Himself as a Sacrifice for many on a wooden cross to redeem the world from sin.

The path to freedom to live our daily lives and worship in Spirit and in Truth is waiting for us in places not occupied by clouds. No longer are we bound to the "Danger Zones" of distraction and control where we cling to illusive preoccupations that "cloud" the path. We are called "Above the Clouds" to live, love and worship freedom in the Spirit. Let us all pray and commit ourselves and the living of these days to "The Unclouded Day."
Thanks be to God.

Reflections

_____

_____

_____

_____

_____

_____

_____

_____

_____

_____

_____

_____

_____

_____

_____

_____

_____

The Divine Dance

There is nary a soul who cannot recall seeing a toddler or even a Facebook post featuring a child's wiggling dance movements in joyful response to music. The sound waves communicate a message to the child's heart and a conversation of pure joy begins. One does not have to be a child to participate in this conversation. Even King David in II Samuel dances with all his might before the Lord, with rejoicing, when bringing up the ark of God to Jerusalem. As children of God and made in His image, all human beings from time to time find themselves in rhythmic movement to the music of the heart - an internal conversation which others cannot hear but only observe the behavioral dialogue.

A song released in 1974 by Rufus and Chaka Khan opens with the words "Tell me something good…Tell me that you love me". Could there be more of a definitive statement regarding the basic need of the human soul? According to C.S. Lewis: "In Christianity, God is not a static thing—not even a person—but a dynamic, pulsating activity, a life, almost a kind of drama. Almost, if you will not think me irreverent, a kind of dance… (The) pattern of this three-personal life is . . . the great fountain of energy and beauty spurting up at the very center of reality."

The fountain of energy and beauty spurting up at the very center of life is God's music. Because the essence of God is love, Love is His music. It is from the heart of the Godhead…that is, from God the Father, God the Son and God the

Holy Spirit. The dynamic conversation amongst the "Three" is eternal in its beauty, energy, affirmation, creativity and love…always addressing the cry of the human soul: "Tell me something good…Tell me that you love me." God the Father, God the Son and God the Holy Spirit forever proclaim: You are worthy, and You are loved!

I am in full agreement with Sam Storms, Christian Author, Teacher and Pastor in his assertion that "God created us so that the joy He has in Himself might be ours. God doesn't simply think about Himself or talk to Himself. He enjoys Himself! He celebrates with infinite and eternal intensity the beauty of who He is as Father, Son, and Holy Spirit. And we've been created to join the party!"

Holy God, we pray that our dance movements in this "party" called the gift of life reflect the love conversation between the Trinity and ourselves as redeemed by Christ.

Reflections

Basic Instructions Before Leaving Earth

With the recent respite in the summer heat wave, I spent the last couple of mornings in the swing on our front porch enjoying cooler temperatures and an occasional waft of refreshing breeze. Even with my seasonal allergies, I could breathe and sing to my Maker in that white wicker swing so reminiscent of many loving times in my life.

I guess it was not by coincidence, when I spoke with a friend of mine later in the day who wanted to know how I was doing, that I responded: "I'm keeping my nose above water and grateful to God to have a nose to breathe." The answer I gave to my friend's question was a decidedly scriptural assessment of my momentary status but not necessarily reflective of the inconsistent ebb and flow in my life of faith. One of the most foundational and challenging teachings from I Thess. 5:18 KJV says: "In everything give thanks, for this is the will of God in Christ Jesus concerning you."

Adherence to this biblical admonition is a needful habit to form in our daily prayers for the formation of our faith but, to be honest, we struggle to believe in our hearts that everything that happens in our lives is the will of God for which we need to give thanks. It is easier to assign blame than to sit in silence and fathom the profound reality of God's love and plans for our lives revealed by hope in Christ Jesus. As human beings, we observe circumstances through a lens of unenlightened selfishness unless we are intentional in our search for faith and understanding as led by the Holy Spirit.

Have you ever heard the song "A Beautiful Morning" by The Rascals from back in the late 1960's? It is a lovely song of comfort and peace written during a time of war and unrest. It begins: "It's a beautiful morning. I think I'll go outside for a while and just smile…Just take in some clean fresh air." I sang this song while sitting on my porch swing…It's comforting imagery has often helped me as I struggle in my daily walk of faith. Even more, God's hopeful promises to the faithful abound in scripture. Psalm 112:4 ESV: "Light dawns in the darkness for the upright; He is gracious, merciful, and righteous." And we are assured from Daniel 12:3 ESV that "those who are wise shall shine like the brightness of the sky above; and those who turn many to righteousness, like the stars forever and ever."

The promise of the Maker and Giver of the Light of the "beautiful morning," is that in consequence of our relationship with Jesus, we will be led to faithful service in spreading the truth of His abiding and transformative love. In the saving grace of His love and power, all believers in Christ can follow the "basic instructions before leaving earth" (B.I.B.L.E.) and pray in obedience and with certainty: "In everything give thanks, for this is the will of God in Christ Jesus concerning you." (KJV)

Lead me kindly light…

One of the earliest memories from my childhood (other than being stung by a yellow-jacket wasp), was one of escaping from imposed isolation. Fleeing this major time-out seemed for me at the time to be critical to my survival as a four-year-old. As a punishment, I had been blocked from re-entry into the house and left enclosed in the fenced area of our backyard. Overwhelmed by the fear this separation represented, I frantically searched for a way out and located a vent in the base of the house foundation. Crawling through the menacing darkness underneath toward the light on the other side, I emerged just a few feet from the kitchen door, which I burst through like a drowning person coming up for air. Without a doubt, this was a formative experience in my life. There was inherent danger in the course of action I pursued. What circumstance was fuel for my desperate behavior? Was it fear or was it actually love?

What has surrounded me all my days has <u>not</u> been an all-pervasive fear leading to darkness and rebellion. Fear of God in the biblical sense refers more often to wonder and awe in bowed submission before God, the King of Creation. The Bible proclaims to us in Proverbs 9:10 CSB that "The fear of the Lord is the beginning of wisdom, and knowledge of the Holy One is understanding". The wisdom of God <u>is</u> God's mind and His words, "Let there be light," birthed creation. God's wisdom <u>is</u> light and, in that light, knowledge and understanding of the Holy One, the Light of the world, is revealed.

Jesus' disciples experienced many instances of darkness, fear and dread…i.e. In the Garden of Gethsemane, at the foot of Jesus' cross, and even outside His empty tomb after the resurrection. All these experiences, which seemed like categoric failures at the time, served to lead them out of darkness and into the light of greater understanding and renewed hope in their Savior and Lord. In

1833, Cardinal John Henry Newman was traveling on a boat returning to his native England, after having been dangerously ill with a fever, when he wrote the hymn, "Lead, Kindly Light. This very popular hymn attests to the comfort and reassurance God gives leading us when we are lost (as did Cardinal Newman himself, when he called on God for strength and his hope was renewed on that journey.) It is the "kindly light" of God's wisdom, love and grace that leads all of mankind to hope in the knowledge and understanding of the Holy One - The Light of the world. There is light at the end of the tunnel…Have you seen the Light?

Reflections

_____

_____

_____

_____

_____

_____

_____

_____

_____

_____

_____

Step and Fetch

The book of Hebrews Chapter 1 verse 14 NIV affirms the answer to the question of the role of angels in our lives: "Are not all angels ministering spirits sent to serve those who will inherit salvation?" The whisper of wings is all around us, if we purpose to listen in quietude in our spirits for their guardianship and governance in our daily lives.

There's a song from the "big band" era made famous by Tommy Dorsey entitled: "On the Sunny Side of the Street." It begins: "Grab your coat and get your hat; Leave your worry on the doorstep. Just direct your feet to the sunny side of the street." It has a unique conclusion: "Gold dust at my feet on the sunny side of the street." Upon review of these lyrics, it occurred to me that it would not be a stretch to use them to illustrate the "step and fetch" notion of angel activities first introduced in the title of this sharing. It delights me to visualize a black and white film like "It's a Wonderful Life." The messenger sent from heaven appears ordinary but accomplishes the extraordinary on behalf of the assigned human…just like having "gold dust at your feet on the sunny side of the street."

I would propose in this metaphorical comparison, that the sunny side of the street represents the love and hope resident in a relationship with Almighty God. The angels are sent from the light of heaven (the sunny side of the street) to share that light and radiance wherever they go and thereby help safeguard lives and direct the behavior of humanity to the "Son." The intervention of the divine for our good is more prevalent than we could ever guess. No believer can deny the overwhelming goodness and tenderness of protection we enjoy because angels "step and fetch" in faithful obedience to the will of the Lord.

I must admit to being resentful in those circumstances when I perceive that I am "expected to step and fetch" without the courtesy of being asked. What a lousy angel I would make with that attitude! But following in the steps of our Servant Lord and the angels He sends in service to us means we should embrace the duties of "step and fetch" in joyful obedience for our good and His glory.

What is that I hear? Could it be the whispering of angel wings?

Reflections

_____

_____

_____

_____

_____

_____

_____

_____

_____

_____

_____

_____

Truth or Dare?

Chartering a WWII bi-plane flown by a former movie stunt pilot would not be my first choice for a fun outing, but the consequence is to miss out on what could be a life-altering experience. The quote: "Danger, Will Robinson!" keeps surfacing in my consciousness as I struggle whether or not to join the excursion.

It's so easy not to try…The easy course of action is to just lie down on my bed and lie to myself that my fear and dread is a reality that cannot be dodged. This fear and dread impacted our lives just recently, in the tragic loss of a friend to a senseless act of violence. More and more people are deciding to just stay home these days, rather than risk the dangers in the outside world.

Yes, the truth is the world can be dangerous, but the world is also a place of beauty and peace made by the Lord Jesus for us. Our Lord and Savior was not dissuaded by the threats of danger and violence against Himself but rather, lived an exemplary life as flesh and blood in this world, with His focus always on the good and well-being of others.

Even though the Son of Man had nowhere to lay His head, He engaged the world He made…teaching the truth, loving and encouraging others, feeding the hungry, healing the sick, and enjoying fellowship in the homes of friends. Jesus likewise endured the condemnation and wrath of the nay-sayers who spread lies about His ministry, and which consequently culminated in His torture and death for the sins of the world.

As joint heirs with Christ, we are here to engage…to teach by example, to enjoy, to love, to give and receive as well as to endure suffering and hardship for the world He made. I am reminded so often of the image of a dog hanging his head out of the back window of a car racing down the road…an image of "pure joy" as he turns his face into the wind to embrace whatever comes.

What a marvelous example for us to turn from our focus on self and trust the embracing wind of "Truth" where our fears take flight. As redeemed souls created by God Almighty, all of us have been freed from fear and lies if we but listen to the Wind of the Spirit in our souls. We are invited into the "Wind" …Wheels up, anyone?

Reflections

_____

_____

_____

_____

_____

_____

_____

_____

_____

_____

_____

_____

Space is opportunity…In the blink of an eye…

Perhaps you might be too young to have heard the song written by Carl Sigman released in 1956 by Perry Como. Some lyrics are: "Dream along with me, I'm on my way to a star; Come along, come along, leave your worries where they are…Up and beyond the sky, watchin' the world roll by, if we go in the right direction, heaven can't be very far."

As this song implies, "space" has always been representative of opportunity, hope and change. Gazing at the night sky, one cannot imagine the boundless occurrences of change happening across the cosmos. In the fraction of a second it takes to blink your eyes, thousands of stars will be born, hundreds will explode and die, millions of planets will form, and our universe will expand by half a million kilometers in diameter…All in the blink of an eye.

Another stark reminder of this phenomenon can be found in the New Testament scripture book of I Corinthians 15:51-54 ESV: "Behold! I tell you a mystery. We shall not all sleep, but we shall all be changed, in a moment, in the twinkling of an eye at the last trumpet. For the trumpet will sound, and the dead will be raised imperishable, and we shall be changed. For this perishable body must put on the imperishable, and this mortal body must put on immortality." The world as we know it will forever change, in the twinkling of an eye.

"Softly and Tenderly," which was originally known as "Softly and Tenderly Jesus is Calling," is a classic invitation hymn from the 19th century. It was written by Will Thompson (1847-1909), who had been inspired to devote himself to writing while attending a meeting by noted evangelist Dwight L. Moody (1837-1899). Later when Moody lay dying in the hospital, he told

Thompson, "Will, I would rather have written 'Softly and Tenderly Jesus Is Calling' than anything I have been able to do in my whole life."

What a testament to a singular contribution to one individual's life! As long as we have breath, the opportunity that space and time represent can be utilized to allow ourselves to be invested by the Holy Spirit to be part of the lyrics of the eternal chorus for the Kingdom of God - "The Final Frontier." May we commit each day to the miracles that <u>can</u> and <u>do</u> occur "in the blink of an eye" through God's Love and Grace.

Reflections

_____

_____

_____

_____

_____

_____

_____

_____

_____

_____

_____

_____

Shake, Rattle and Roll…Shall We Dance?

In Chapter 37:1-10 KJV of the Old Testament book of Ezekiel, (the name Ezekiel meaning, "God strengthens"), there is a graphic story about the valley of the dry bones. As God's Spirit leads Ezekiel through the valley, he is instructed to prophesy over the bones that they will come to life! The bones literally, "shake, rattle and roll"- joining together with muscle, skin and sinew forming over them.

Elvis' rendition of the song title I usurped for this week's Sharing has the lyrics: "Get out of that bed, wash your face and hands; Get in that kitchen, make some noise with the pots and pans. Shake, rattle and roll; Shake, rattle and roll." Not a bad way to refer to the dry bones of lethargy I endured for the last few days as I lay in the bed and/or sat on the couch laboring to discover the scriptural theme for my Sunday Sharing. Like Ezekiel's discourse with God when He asked Ezekiel if the bones could be restored, God was really asking if Ezekiel had faith in Him to restore the bones. With the help of God's Spirit, I had to speak over my dry spiritual bones in faith and believe that life would indeed return to them.

I am so grateful to be able to witness this prophecy in my life. Things in need of resuscitation in my life (and in all our lives) can be restored with the breath of new life if we trust our Lord and Maker. Of paramount importance is to continue learning to wait on the Lord Who promises to supply all our need according to His riches in glory by Christ Jesus.(Philippians 4:19 NIV) As we wait on the dance floor of life, let's take the extended hand of the Lord Who asks us to join in the dance and trust He will strengthen us to follow His lead…"Shall we dance?"

Reflections

The Nitty Gritty… "Listen to your life"

This past Monday, Aug. 15, 2022, the world mourned the loss of Frederick Buechner, known as inspired Christian "Writer's Writer" and "Minister's Minister." When asked on numerous occasions what was the nitty gritty sum of his writings and preaching spanning over six decades, he always answered: "Listen to your life"

The "nitty gritty" is the essential substance, basics or crux of a matter. But how does one listen to their life? It is not like sitting on the sofa with popcorn and watching a video unfold. It is more like tuning-in to a station on the radio. To clarify…One can: Tune-in, be aware of, and become sensitive to certain incoming material; Tune-out…block incoming discourse and stop paying attention; or Tune-up in preparation. Each of us has the choice to tune-in, tune-out and tune-up in response to the fabric of truths, lies or distractions that we face in this world.

In John Chapter 3, we find the story of the Pharisee, Nicodemus (meaning Victory of the People), a ruler of the Jews. His tradition was positioned against the teaching that Jesus was the Son of God. He came to Jesus under cover of night to question and delve into the nature and particulars of Jesus' calling. Jesus answered him: "And this is the condemnation, that light is come into the world, and men loved darkness rather than light, because their deeds were evil. For everyone that doeth evil hateth the light, neither cometh to the light, lest his deeds should be reproved. But he that doeth truth cometh to the light, that his deeds may be made manifest, that they are wrought in God."
(John 3:19-21 KJV)

Nicodemus went out searching after midnight to try to tune-in to the message of truth. Many others around him had tuned-out…they had lost their head lamps and became twisted-up in the darkness of a nitty gritty existence, for lack of revelation knowledge of the divine Son of Man. If we "listen to the life" of Nicodemus we will hear its "tuning-up," as he made himself present after the crucifixion of Jesus, providing the customary embalming spices, and assisting Joseph of Arimathea in preparing the body of Jesus for burial (John19:39-42 KJV).

Are we tuned-in, and tuned-up or are we tuned-out to the divine message and calling on our lives? When you "listen to your life" is the nitty gritty crux of your life the Cross of Christ? The song is tuned-in and broadcasting on the divine station: "Come to Jesus and Live".

Reflections

Mixed Messages… "Choose you this day…"

Have you ever heard someone ask: "Can I help you?", when that is not what they meant at all. Rather, they were communicating irritation at being interrupted or that their personal space had been intruded upon. Likewise, the exclamation "Excuse me!" might just as often refer to a similar circumstance of irritation and not a platitude of politeness. We live in a world rife with complexity in mixed messaging - almost sublingual (underside of the tongue) in tone and application.

Most recently, I received a mixed message at my doctor's appointment. On the one hand, I weighed fourteen pounds less than on my last visit more than two years ago, which was good news. This good report, however, was off-set by lab results which indicated a high cholesterol level…not the good kind. I puzzled as to how to interpret the import of these two messages which seemed to me to be diverse in nature. However true the weight loss, I was still left with choices to make regarding changes in eating habits to reduce unhealthy cholesterol levels. In effect, without behavioral changes, I will be weighed down by the consequences of my choices.

In the Garden of Eden, Adam and Eve also found themselves burdened by the weight of their choices. The first question asked by God in the Bible is found in Genesis 3:9 AMP: "Where are you?" God asked as He sought Adam and Eve. In truth, it was a mixed message, but one of monumental importance and revelation. Implicit in the question are soul searching topics regarding disobedience and its consequences but also the nature of God Himself.

A quote from Vincent van Gogh is applicable here: "Conscience is a man's compass." Of course, Adam and Eve were not lost in the geographic sense.

They had hidden themselves from God because of the weight of guilt and shame. But the Lord God knew exactly where they were and sought them to provide restoration, when He foretold the plan of salvation in Genesis 3:15. The compass of Adam and Eve's consciences was askew - true north, that is, the truth gleaned from a conscience cleansed by the blood of the Lamb could not register in their souls at this point in time. Only later, through the life and blood sacrifice of Christ for the sins of mankind would the compass dial of a "good" conscience be restored. (For the Son of Man is come to seek and save that which was lost. Luke 19:10 KJV)

"Where are you?" God asks (Genesis 3:8-10 AMP.) Are you weighed down and hiding in shame as a consequence of your choices? Chapter 12 of the book of Hebrews ASV admonishes us to "lay aside every weight, and the sin which doth so easily beset us." The weight of the sin of mankind was borne by Jesus but His "Grace" is free from burden and weight.

Has your soul been freed by grace from the weight of wrong choices, excuses and mixed messages? Or better said…How much does your soul weigh?

3 Little Birds On Granny's Path

There is a country road we pass each week in our travels called Granny's Path. This road is small and nondescript just as the name suggests, but it has always caught my attention. I find my thoughts routinely drifting to my mother and grandmother, whose lives, ways and demeanor had such profound power over the person I thought I was and would eventually become. The natural state is that as human beings, we are shaped and influenced by our surroundings, our environment and other proximal individuals such as family, friends and traditional cultures and norms. The parents of Christ were supernaturally chosen to garner the best for His earthly familial life. But even Jesus, "the Word made flesh," found His path more authentically in the temple. Luke 2:49 (TPT) "Jesus said to them, 'Why would you need to search for me? Didn't you know that it was necessary for me to be here in my Father's house, consumed with Him?'"

In spite of the abundant sources of examples of faith and hope added to the daily mix in my life growing up (albeit less than perfect), I wrestled with overwhelming feelings of loneliness for as long as I can remember. Spending time in the Word revealed to me that the Lord Jesus spent much of His life alone. But He was not alone…In prayerful isolation from humanity, Christ was not separated from His Father. His time spent alone with God the Father was essential to His Divine Calling. Whether in seclusion on a mountain top, the Temptation in the Wilderness or the Garden of Gethsemane, Jesus sought to be alone in communion with God. Not until His crucifixion, when He cried: "My God, my God, why hast Thou forsaken me?" (Matt.27:46 KJV) did the Savior of the world experience separation from His Father. As the One and Only Sinless Lamb of God, Jesus experienced the excruciating and fundamental pain of being "truly alone." This would be an opportune time to share a portion of a favorite creed from the United Church of Canada (1968): "We are not alone, we live in God's world. We believe in God Who has created and is creating, who has come in Jesus, the Word made flesh, to reconcile and make new, who works in us and others by the Spirit. We trust in God…In life, in death, in life beyond death, God is with us. We are not alone."

I am also reminded of a song by Jamaican singer/songwriter, Bob Marley from the late 1970's. Its' lyrics repeat over and over: "Don't worry about a thing, 'cause every little thing is gonna be alright." Oddly enough, the title of the song is Three Little Birds. There are 2 stories regarding the origin of the song title…it is said that three canaries would often come and serenade Bob Marley on his doorstep or another story promotes the back-up singers as the Three Little Birds. I prefer to view the Three Little Birds as The Father, The Son and The Holy Spirit Who serenade the beloved in eternal loving Presence so that we are never alone. "In life, in death, in life beyond death, God is with us. We are not alone." Elvis has left the building, but God is in the room with me, so "every little thing is gonna be all right." I am not alone…You are not alone. The 3 Little Birds are with us on all the Granny's Paths of our lives.
Thanks be to God.

Seascape by Daniel Bonnell

Sad Eyes…Open the Floodgates of Heaven

The world in which we wake each morning is a wild mix of earth and sky, stone and spirit, love and hate, beauty and despair and light and darkness. This is the arena of God's love for us, much of which we did not choose…or did we?

The book of Genesis Chapter 6 NIV, recounts what the state of the heart of mankind had become as a result of their choices: "The Lord saw how great the wickedness of the human race had become on the earth, and that every inclination of the thoughts of the human heart was only evil all the time. The Lord regretted that he had made human beings on the earth, and his heart was deeply troubled." The "Sad Eyes" of the Lord saw how corrupt the world had become and His Eyes overflowed with tears in such fashion, that the earth was flooded, and all its inhabitants lost, save Noah and those sheltered in the ark.

In Hebrews 4:15 KJV, the "sad eyes" of the Lord reveal He is "touched with the feeling of our infirmities." There are three New Testament accounts that Jesus wept: At the tomb of Lazarus (John 11:35 KJV), Over Jerusalem (Luke 19:41 AMP) and at the end of His life in prayer to the One Who could save Him from death (Hebrews 5:7-9 KJV). Jesus wept over the inability of those He had come to save to see the truth. Just as in the story of Noah and the flood and the life of love and sacrifice of His dear Son for all mankind, The Lord's response is always to open the floodgates of heaven to cleanse and make new.

It has been said that "whoever holds the gun is god until he pulls the trigger - then he is the devil." In my city this week and across the nation and globe, there has been so much violence, loss of life and injustice. But it is how we respond as we face the contradictions and challenges of this world that make a difference. God did not leave us without hope. There's always light behind the clouds…the notable placement of a rainbow after the flood warrants attention.

This journey in God's arena of love is also one of blessing. I would be remiss in not mentioning that although we mourn the passing of the beloved 96-year-old Queen Elizabeth II this week, we can be comforted by her words of wisdom: "We sometimes think the world's problems are so big that we can do little to help. On our own, we cannot end wars or wipe-out injustice but the cumulative impact of thousands of small acts of goodness can be bigger than we imagine." A sparkling rainbow appeared in the sky over London and Buckingham Palace shortly after the announcement of the passing of this great servant of God to the well-being of mankind.

Somewhere over the rainbow, as well as, in the here and now, "Sad eyes" are ones that "know" the truth and respond in the love and light of heaven behind the clouds. May we make faithful choices which lead the floodgates of the mercy and grace of heaven to be open to us. For it is in Jesus' Name and because He lives, we pray. Amen.

Reflections

To Blame is Lame…Rather, Exclaim the Name!

"Well, here's another nice mess you've gotten me into!" A famous line from many of the escapades of the Laurel and Hardy movies was when Hardy routinely blamed Laurel for their predicament. He never blamed himself or other dark souls around them with hidden agendas…and certainly not God.

It is a unique quality of human nature to blame others for our mistakes. In the beginning, even Adam blamed God in Genesis 3:12-13 AMP for giving him the woman - Eve, who caused his disobedience by giving him the forbidden fruit to eat; Eve then pointed the finger and blamed the serpent for tricking her, thus causing her to disobey God. Even Moses, in Exodus 17 ESV, blamed the Israelites for making him angry, causing him to disobey God, when he struck the rock to provide water for the people, instead of speaking to it…And the list goes on throughout recorded history of the prominence of the blame game in our societies.

We blame other people, and we blame God as well for our lot in life. However, there is a contrast to the blame game in which human beings become frequently engaged. Ofttimes, we utter a different cry when something alarming happens. Whether believer or not, the first thing most people say is, "Jesus!" I have to admit that hearing this exclamation, upon being faced with a distressful situation, does not sound like the blaming of God, but more of a desperate plea for help. That would seem evidential support of biblical teaching that we are all made in the image and likeness of God. Without a moment's reflection, the human spirit instinctively cries out to its Lord and Savior, regardless of theological or non-theological tradition.

There is power in the name of Jesus. Phil. 2:9-10 KJV proclaims: "Wherefore God also hath highly exalted him and given him a name which is above every name: That at the name of Jesus every knee should bow…" Whatsoever ye shall ask in my name, that will I do, that the Father may be glorified in the Son." (John 14:13 KJV) A Traditional Gospel song by Tasha Cobbs Leonard released in 2013 entitled: Break Every Chain" lauds the potency of Jesus' name when invoked to address the needs of the world. It begins: "There is power in the name of Jesus; To break every chain, break every chain, break every chain." (Ps. 107:13-16 NIV: "They cried to the Lord in their trouble, and he saved them from their distress. He brought them out of darkness, the utter darkness, and broke away their chains.")

Some would cast speculation on this aforementioned practice of exclaiming "Jesus" when in the throes of threat or fear as almost an example of blasphemy or heresy. The holy scriptures attest otherwise…Exclaim His Name! "There is power in the Name of Jesus to break every chain!" Thanks be to God.

The "Wrong" Stuff vs. The "Right Stuff"

"But this is the way we've always done it!" is a commonly used justification. My husband met this response when he suggested a change in a church board meeting agenda. The first hour was devoted to finances, i.e., discussion of the cost of toilet paper and similar supplies for the church which routinely led to wasted time and even argument. He proposed that the mission of the church (to its members and outside the church walls) should open the meeting, leaving the details regarding the prices of toilet paper, etc. to the end of the meeting.

In "Freedom for Ministry" Richard John Neuhaus, who was a prominent Christian cleric and writer, addresses the church and its mission. Perhaps he is the one who coined this phrase from his book: "the thus and so-ness of the church." The status quo is "thus," therefore what comes after thus is "so," i.e.., Thus...., so.... The "so" is built on the foundation of "thus." Business as usual should never be the regulating force in the church.

During the time of Christ on this earth, Pharisees and Sadducees, leaders of the Jewish faith, knew well the value of "business as usual" to protect and defend against change. To the religious leaders, Jesus represented a threat to the faith and not enlightenment. The Messiah made this indictment of them: "Woe to you, teachers of the law and Pharisees, you hypocrites! You shut the kingdom of heaven in men's faces. You yourselves do "not enter, nor will you let those enter who are trying to." (Matthew 23:27 NIV)

What is the basis of resistance to the consideration of change in organizations? To quote Father Neuhaus, "In the absence of truth, power is the only game in town." The Pharisees and Sadducees thought they had the only game in town. They were all too familiar with posturing, so that ordinances appeared to be upheld in their lives by their actions. They lacked revelation knowledge of "The Truth" however, and they could not be counted as righteous - their hearts were unchanged.

Holding on to power (the "Wrong Stuff") has been quite the familiar platform throughout the history of the world. Followers of the truth of Christ must reject this human tendency for holding on to power and be prepared to embrace Spirit-driven change. But how to accomplish this call to our lives by our Savior means we must exercise love in sharing the truth of needed changes and reforms to others in our leadership roles in the church. Apart from the path of "love" we will be deniers of truth and guilty of being hypocrites just like the Pharisees.

May our heart's prayer be to commit to the "Right Stuff" - the path of "Love" and let that commitment serve to transform the "thus and so-ness of the church" into dynamic Spirit-led change. In Christ's Name we pray and for the sake of His Kingdom. Amen.

Walk it, Talk it in Your Heart -
Then, Come Home…Softly and Tenderly

We have all heard the phrase, "Walk a mile in my shoes," an admonition to exercise restraint before passing judgment on another. In preparation for our vacation this Fall to South Dakota and Wounded Knee Reservation, I chanced upon a similar quote: "Walk a Mile in His Moccasins," a famous quoted line from a poem written in 1895 by Mary T. Lathrap, an American poet and licensed preacher in the Methodist Episcopal Church.

A noted story in Old Testament Scripture comes to mind of the tale of Sodom and Gomorrah. Lot's wife looked backward over her shoulder at the burning destruction while she, her husband and two daughters were fleeing the city of Sodom. Having been warned, she nonetheless looked behind in regret over the loss of the life she was leaving and was subsequently turned into a pillar of salt. (Genesis 19:15-26 NIV)

In all fairness, how many of us as human beings and believers have not acted in likewise fashion, looking backward with feelings of regret and loss instead of focusing on the promises of God on the path before us. The question remains: How do we live obedient lives of discernment as Christians and yet not be guilty of judging? The answer can be articulated in the words of the original title of Mary Lathrap's poem, that is, "Judge Softly."

Galatians 5:22-23 CSB tells us that the fruits of the Spirit are love, joy, peace, patience, kindness, goodness, faithfulness, gentleness, and self-control. What a different world we would live in each day if our judging was softer and tempered with love, patience, kindness and gentleness. In order to walk a mile in someone's shoes, albeit moccasins, we must first walk it and talk it in our hearts and then walk it and talk it in our lives, through the fruits of the Spirit, not the least of which is self-control.

But how do we softly and tenderly exercise self-control at the same time we make our protestations over injustice? II Timothy 2:24-25 NKJV teaches that "a servant of the Lord must not quarrel but be gentle to all, able to teach, patient, in humility correcting those who are in opposition, if God perhaps will grant them repentance, so that they may know the truth."

Heavenly Father, lead us in Your gentle way of "judging softly." May our prayer always be to live our lives in such a way that we Come Home…Softly and Tenderly.

Mirror, mirror…

What does a saint look like?

Through images in statues and paintings, we have come to recognize over the centuries those persons the church has deemed as Saints. Even the Son of man has been thusly depicted, yet no one really knows what Jesus looked like unless they met Him in person on earth or in heaven. But again, there is the question: What does a saint look like…Isn't it plausible to think that someone so venerated by the church could be readily identified? Or shouldn't a person committed to the love of Christ, though unheralded as a saint, be identified as such when doing the work for the Kingdom of God.

Have you ever seen yourself in a mirror and been startled at the reflection returning the gaze? Not due to lack of make-up or frizzy hair, it is my opinion that this odd circumstance can be credited to the habit of depending on others for a definition of self. Perhaps it is a diffident or lackadaisical approach to living but nonetheless, it is the fall-back position for humans to lose sight of themselves when enveloped in their perception by a stronger personality.

The "good news" is that God calls you a saint if you are a follower of Christ, having received salvation through faith in His sacrificial gift of love and grace. The believer in Christ is dominated by His strong personhood - The Spirit of God resides in the hearts of believers and that image is reflected back when we view ourselves in the mirror of our daily walk with Him. The scriptures espouse that through time spent in the Word of God and in prayer and confession, we will see through the glass darkly but there will be a time when we see "face to face".

The Living Bible paraphrases I Corinthians 13:12 TLB as follows: "In the same way, we can see and understand only a little about God now, as if we were peering at his reflection in a poor mirror; but someday we are going to see him in his completeness, face-to-face. Now all that I know is hazy and blurred, but then I will see everything clearly, just as clearly as God sees into my heart right now." The more we seek Christ, the more His image is reflected from ourselves to the world - even to ourselves. And although we see an unclear image when we look in the mirror, it nonetheless reveals the sustaining core of our hearts. Mirror, mirror on the wall…Who's the fairest one of all? *Fairest Lord Jesus*

Reflections

_____

_____

_____

_____

_____

_____

_____

_____

_____

_____

When "Lest" is "More"

It is, and has always been thus, that some do not possess the advantages of others. All of us encounter persons on the exit ramp of the expressway or a favored intersection that has a regular population of sign-holders..."Anything helps!" They lift up the signs in their arms in hope of support. It is difficult not to stop and pass a bit of currency out the window. There are arguments on both sides... "Is the need real, or just a ploy to fund a drug or alcohol addiction?" "And besides, aren't there shelters, churches and government programs in place to help those in need." Offering a blind eye to the situation is a choice many of us make so that our internal discomfort and dialogue is silenced.

In the plea "Alms for the poor" the term "alms" originated from the Greek word "eleos" meaning mercy. From ancient times, Almsgiving is food, money or assistance offered in love. "Alms for the poor" reverberates silently in our minds and hearts but perhaps not. The signage and/or the tin cups are lifted by the arms of those seeking aid. These cups can likewise be filled with change if we but extend our arms of support to be agents of our God to fill them. Scripture offers many instances of cups needing filling. There is even a song by Richard Blanchard which cries "Fill my cup, Lord; I lift it up, Lord. Come and quench this thirsting of my soul."

It would seem that "alms and arms" are linked by God from the beginning. To be that agent of change we must provide the change in the uplifted cup but in order to do so, we must be first changed in our perspective... "Judge not, lest ye be judged." (Matthew 7:1) is an appropriate scriptural application here. "Lest would indeed be more" when we cease to judge and instead lend our supportive arms to give alms. We can no longer turn a blind eye to a situation, perhaps feigning itself as urgent, but be willing to endure whatever discomfort there may be in loving sacrifice to the truthful ways of God.

Just recently, I had the opportunity to order a stained-glass window. It was marketed with two finishes - one was called "opalescent" because light is blocked from shining through it. The other choice was "cathedral" finish because it allows the light to be filtered through the window. As instruments of God's grace in this world, may we see through the windows of our souls as through "cathedral" panes of love, light and compassion. Amen.

Reflections

_____

_____

_____

_____

_____

_____

_____

_____

_____

Wound Care...
Beyond Band-aids

Wound care has been on my mind this week. Just recently, we ate dinner with friends in their home. Our small dog, who is always welcome there, accompanied us for the occasion. I made an error in judgment during the meal and reached down to pick up my pet and place her in my lap. She slipped from my grip and her claws accidentally made a deep and bloody cut on my forearm. My friends, both of whom are doctors, immediately shot out of their chairs to help address the wound and remedy the situation.

Some wounds, however, are "beyond band-aids" to remedy successfully. We are admonished in scripture to bind each other's wounds, but many wounds are unseen in this world. Moreover, how do we help others and ourselves to address the wounds that are self-inflicted? From his song "Anthem," author, Leonard Cohen sings, "There is a crack, a crack in everything. That's how the light gets in." These lyrics are often summarized: "We are all broken but that is how the light gets in!" What are wounds, if not cracks and broken places in our bodies and spirits which God, in the light of His love, can heal.

The Apostle Paul reveals God's prescriptive light: "In everything give thanks: for this is the will of God in Christ Jesus concerning you." I Thessalonians 5:18 KJV. All of us find ourselves facing difficult and dangerous situations. Even our Lord Christ, who was fully human and fully divine, prayed in the Garden of Gethsemane before He was arrested: "Father, if Thou be willing, remove this cup from me: nevertheless, not my will, but Thine, be done." Luke 22:42 KJV) And there is further enlightenment in I Thessalonians Chapter 5:16-18 KJV, which contains far more than a list of platitudes...Paul also admonishes to

"Rejoice evermore" and "Pray without ceasing," the practice of which helps set the climate of the womb of our daily lives.

When we find ourselves "in" a "nevertheless" womb of trial in life, scripture admonishes us to "give" thanks. This is a proactive gesture of obedience which activates the faith mechanism of the Spirit to strengthen and propel the believer through painful circumstances. In this way, we are birthed from focus and orientation on ourselves into the light of God's love and resources and we, as believers, are postured to recognize and help bind the wounds of others in this world. Thus, as we are continually birthed and re-birthed from the womb of trial, the intuition and wisdom of the Spirit is channeled to comfort and mend "beyond band-aids" to the Glory of God and His everlasting kingdom of love and light. Let us…nevertheless.

Reflections

What did Jesus do?

How did Jesus respond to abuse?

He spoke the truth in love and He turned the other cheek; He did good to those that hated him; He forgave seventy times seven and more to those that harmed Him; He gave soft answers and turned away wrath.

The idiom "knee jerk reaction" or automatic reaction was coined in the late 19th century, referring to the sudden involuntary extension of the leg in response to a light blow just below the knee (also known as the patellar reflex). I have often been perplexed as to the existence and/or non-existence of these automatic reactions in my spiritual life. One would hope that a mature faith walk would garner more positive "knee jerk reactions" to people and circumstances than negative ones. More often than I would care to admit, negative feelings and unloving reactions to people and situations swarm about and steal my peace.

Through the grace of God, I have found that the disturbance of my peace brings a "good" pain. But can pain really be a good thing? Most people have experienced that prickling feeling from the slow return of blood flow to a limb that has gone to sleep. Although it is uncomfortable, the sheer awareness and increase of the prickling pain is assurance of abiding health, i.e., the pain is necessary to return strength to the body part. I liken this physical experience to a faith counterpart confirmed in James 1:3-4 NIV "Because you know that the testing of your faith produces perseverance, Let perseverance finish its work so that you may be mature and complete, not lacking anything."

To endure the pain of testing does require a loving and faithful response from the believer in Christ. Firstly, the "knee jerk" reaction must be replaced from one of offense and payback to a "love response." This first step demands submitting what seems to be a humanly justified response to the example and teachings of Jesus…For us, His followers, that means denying the flesh. The reward of peace to faithful perseverance awaits those who routinely and successfully say "no" to their flesh. Focus on the "self" must be transferred to focus on the "Love" of God in His Savior Christ, through the Spirit's power.

What would Jesus do?   Whatever "Love" requires.

Reflections

Devoted or Divided?

There are common seeds to both commitments in life. It is the fruit of the planted seed that has significance in the perspective of eternity. As created beings with carnal natures bent on sinning, we are all in this together. Receiving the gift of salvation into our spirits does not erase (for the present) the residual filth of the sin nature. Our zeal and devotion to walk the higher sanctified path leads us at times to become discerning filters of the filth. But is it necessary to get down and dirty to clean it? Jesus didn't think so...

(John 8:1-11 KJV)

"Jesus went unto the mount of Olives. And early in the morning he came again into the temple, and all the people came unto him; and he sat down and taught them. And the scribes and Pharisees brought unto him a woman taken in adultery; and when they had set her in the midst, They say unto him, Master, this woman was taken in adultery, in the very act. Now Moses in the law commanded us, that such should be stoned: but what sayest thou? This they said, tempting him, that they might have to accuse him. But Jesus stooped down, and with his finger wrote on the ground, as though he heard them not. So when they continued asking him, he lifted up himself, and said unto them, He that is without sin among you, let him first cast a stone at her. And again, he stooped down, and wrote on the ground. And they which heard it, being convicted by their own conscience, went out one by one, beginning at the eldest, even unto the last: and Jesus was left alone, and the woman standing in the midst. When Jesus had lifted up himself, and saw none but the woman, he said unto her, Woman, where are those thine accusers? hath no man condemned thee? She said, No man, Lord. And Jesus said unto her, Neither do I condemn thee: go, and sin no more."

Jesus did not disavow the law, nor did He take sides with the adulterous behavior. (Let me say at this time, it is interesting that the instance the scribes and Pharisees used to trap Jesus was adultery, when any behavior which disavows the pledge of devotion is considered adulterous in nature) Jesus did not respond in judgment of the act - Nor did He soil Himself contributing to division. He only dirtied Himself by drawing in the dirt on the ground with His finger. Please note: Jesus' finger was not pointed at anyone - just pointed toward the ground from which those present (both accusers and accused) came from and would one day return. He offered a different path of enlightenment when He said: "He that is without sin among you, let him first cast a stone at her." It was the path of divine love and forgiveness for her and for all of us guilty of adulterous ways regarding our devotion to God and His gift of eternal life to humanity: "Neither do I condemn thee: go, and sin no more."

Let us commit to follow Jesus' example of devotion to God and forgiveness and inclusion so as not to plant seeds bearing unrighteous fruit.

Christ's testimony is: I am yours and you are Mine.

"Blest be the Tie that binds our hearts in Christian love."

The "Joy" Road and The 4 "R's"

Walking the "Joy Road" in joyful obedience is founded on the Word of God. Scripture is telling, regarding Christ's path of obedience in Hebrews 12:2 KJV: "Looking unto Jesus the author and finisher of our faith; who for the joy that was set before him endured the cross, despising the shame, and is set down at the right hand of the throne of God." Unlike our Lord Christ, I don't remember being full of joy when obeying my parents or other persons in authority when I was growing up. I would be remiss in not sharing that there were times it made me feel good to have pleased my parents by obeying, but mostly, it felt like a tedious duty about which I had no choice. I wonder how many of us who call ourselves Christians really feel we are traveling the "Joy" Road. Is there such a thing as joyful obedience or are we just proceeding on…trying to fake it until we make it?

In the Greek language, the word translated "to rejoice" literally means to be favorably disposed to God's grace. But without the revelation of the truth of God's Word, one can't be "favorably disposed to God's grace" or free to commit to walk in joyful obedience on the road of faith. One of the most famous highways in our nation is Route 66 which has been a setting of character featured in movies and tv series alike. In his novel, The Grapes of Wrath 1939, John Steinbeck referred to Route 66 as "The Mother Road" - a road of hope for a new beginning - A "Joy Road" of sorts, where the hope of joy is birthed.

In all matters of life, the root is the source from which life emerges. We see in Hebrews 12:2 KJV that obedience and love are in relationship and resident in that relationship, love is the root source of joyful obedience. The Love of God as revealed in Christ Jesus is the "**Root**" and His path is the "**Route**". Also requisite in the "Route" is "**Right**" as in one's choice and manner of following the "Route."

Hence, the three R's, but not like what we learned in grade school. Inherent in this classroom is the quality of being "**Ripe**" with humility - the fourth "R." Humility is unassuming and demonstrates a warm attitude toward others. On the other hand, to be prideful shows focus on self so there is no human warmth to share. Those persons living in pride are standing tall in stature in their own perspective, with heads held high. Whereas, the humble do not regard themselves first, but live as with heads bowed, favorably disposed to God's grace.

Regardless of terrain, we journey on the "Mother Road" birthed from God's "**Root**" of Love; we are committed to His "**Route**" of following "**Right**"; and finally, "**Ripe**" with humility, we offer a canopy of mercy, grace, joy, love, forgiveness and peace to the world. God can only lift our heads to see Him when our heads are first lowered in humility. As followers of Christ, the true "Joy Road" in life can only be found in humble obedience to the Love of God. When questioned in the classroom about the **4 "R's,"** may all of us sojourners in the faith eagerly raise our hands in affirmation and say: "I know teacher!"

All Saints Day

The Wishing Well by Connie Dover
Lyrics Adapted from Padraic Pearse's, *Renunciation* by Connie Dover
Additional verses by Lana Lee Marler

When first I saw you, I saw beauty,
And I blinded my eyes,
For fear that I should weep.

When first I heard you, I heard sweetness,
And I turned away,
For fear of my weakness.

I blinded my eyes, My face I turned away,
I hardened my heart for fear of my ruin.

But your love, my Lord, I cannot forsake,
Silent tears wash my soul, A vow I would make.

I opened my eyes; My face turned not away,
Purest joy fills my heart,
I rest in your embrace.

https://heavens.jacobsladdercdc.org/home/wishing

Who is my brother? Thou knowest...

Shaking hands has been the greeting of respect and deference since medieval times. It communicates in gesture more than time allows for in words. For many today in our contemporary culture, the fist bump or offering a bent elbow has supplanted the traditional handshake – a shorthand embrace, yet nonetheless effective in communicating brotherly connection. But who is my brother? A brother is someone with whom there is connection and understanding. A brother consistently offers a listening ear.

If a person with no faith background asked you: "How do I talk to God? The simple truthful response is: "Just talk – God is always listening." You don't have to be in a church or any certain setting to make the connection.   David testifies to the nature of our relationship with our God in Psalm 139:2; 4 (KJV) 2 "Thou knowest my downsitting and mine uprising, thou understandest my thought afar off. 4 For [there is] not a word in my tongue, [but], lo, O LORD, thou knowest it altogether. "

More often than not, the prayer words I offer when I talk to God are: "Thou knowest." Comforting scripture passages abound…"For thou, Lord GOD, knowest thy servant." (II Samuel 7:20); "Thou knowest my foolishness; and my sins are not hid from thee." (Psalm 69:5); "Hear Thou from heaven Thy dwelling place, and forgive, and render unto every man, for Thou only knowest the hearts of the children of men." (II Chronicles 6:30) Even the Apostle Peter who thrice denied knowing Christ at His crucifixion is recorded in the gospel of John 21:17: "And he said unto Him, Lord, Thou knowest all things; Thou knowest that I love Thee. "

May I proffer once again: The shorthand prayer which helps provide understanding, comfort, connection and healing to my life is: "Thou knowest." It is offered in faith to the listening ear of God and to Whom I ask: "Who is my brother?" Without fail, God's fist bump brotherly response to me is: "Thou knowest." "Feed my sheep."

Christ the King

Any Day Now by Lana Lee Marler

Any day now, my heart will hear God say,
'Now is the time,' My Son is on the way;"
This bird loosed from its cage, no more to roam.
Any day now, my God will call me home.

Any day now, changed in the twinkling of an eye;
At the trump sound and to my glad surprise;
Then the love beams will fall from heaven to the ground.
Any day now, I will not be around.

Loved ones, He's coming soon, our Savior;
And we shall meet Him in the air;
To live and sing his praise until forever.
No more holding on to this life as before.

Any day now, with all those called by His name;
Quickly I'll rise, there's no more tears or pain;
This bird loosed from its cage, no more to roam.
Any day now, God's love will bid me, 'Come!'

Loved ones, He's coming soon, our Savior;
And we shall meet Him in the air;
To live and sing his praise until forever.
No more holding on to this life as before.

Then the love beams will fall from heaven to the ground;
And we shall meet Him in the air;
To live and sing His praise until forever.
Any day now, Any day now… We're heaven bound.

https://heavens.jacobsladdercdc.org/home/any

Not if, but when…Some things are certain.

There is a popular hymn written in 1941 by Esther Kerr Rusthoi entitled, "When We See Christ" which is a testament to the title of this meditation. Perhaps you are familiar with the refrain: "It will be worth it all, when we see Jesus; Life's trials will seem so small, when we see Christ. One glimpse of His dear face, all sorrow will erase; So, bravely run the race, 'til we see Christ."

We had a clergyman friend years ago who had a unique sense of humor. He had endured his share of hard knocks in life but by and large used jokes to filter his responses to them. I remember his sharing that while growing up, he thought his full name was David Listen because that is how most often, he was addressed at home: "David, Listen!! Despite this stubborn streak and less than perfect upbringing situation, he listened and answered the call of God. But having committed his life to God and the church, it was a difficult circumstance to face the inevitable reality of coming up short in his Christian example. Referring to the aforementioned song in wavering faith, he used to misquote the lyrics, saying: "It will be worth it all, **if** we see Jesus." This would always bring a pained smile to the listener in affirmation of a similar faith challenge while affording our clergyman friend a moment of shared confession.

"It will be worth it all when we see Christ" is the reality for all believers in contrast to the misquotation **"if"** we see Christ. Some things are certain…Not "if" but "when." All will stand before the judgment seat of Christ but be comforted and remember the words of the apostle, James: "Blessed is the man who remains steadfast under trial, for when he has stood the test he will receive the crown of life, which God has promised to those who love him" (James 1:12).   "For I know the plans I have for you," declares the Lord, "plans to prosper you and not to harm you, plans to give you hope and a future." (Jeremiah 29:11) Some things are certain…The crown of eternal life is our hope and future. Let us determine to **"Listen."**

Reflections

_____

_____

_____

_____

_____

_____

_____

_____

_____

_____

_____

Reflections

_____

_____

_____

_____

_____

_____

_____

_____

_____

_____

_____

_____

_____

_____

_____

_____

_____

Reflections

_____

_____

_____

_____

_____

_____

_____

_____

_____

_____

_____

_____

_____

_____

_____

_____

References

Cold feet...Having done all to stand

[Author Unknown]., [n.d]., *Standing in the Need of Prayer* [online] Hymnary.org. Available at: https://hymnary.org/text/not_my_brother_nor_my_sister_but_its_me

It's so easy not to try…It's not so easy not to cry
The Return of the King., 1980. [film] *It's so easy not to try.* [online] Director Rankin, Jr, Author, Japan and USA

The still small voice, When small is anything but…
Vonnegut, Kurt, Jr., (n.d.). *Enjoy the little things in life...* [online] Goodreads.com. Available at: https://www.goodreads.com/quotes/471392-enjoy-the-little-things-in-life-because-one-day-you-ll
Winner, Septimus., 1868. *Whispering Hope.* [online] Hymnary.org. Available at: https://hymnary.org/text/soft_as_the_voice_of_an_angel

Stand and Deliver! "Mary, did you know?"
Greene, Buddy, Lowry, Mark., 1996. *Mary, Did You Know?* [online] Hymnary.org. Available at: https://hymnary.org/tune/mary_did_you_know

No More Power Outages
Jones, Lewis E., 1899. *Power in the Blood* [online] Hymnary.org. Available at: https://hymnary.org/text/would_you_be_free_from_the_burden_jones

In His Steps
Chisholm, Thomas O., 1923. *Great is Thy Faithfulness* [online] Hymnary.org. Available at: https://hymnary.org/text/great_is_thy_faithfulness_o_god_my_fathe

Being There
Being There. 1979. [film] Directed by Hal Ashby. Asheville, North Carolina, USA. BSB, CIP, and Lorimar Film Entertainment

Sing to the Lord a New Song (Ps. 96:1)
Gandhi, Mahatma. (n.d.). *"The day the power of love overrules the love of power, the world will know peace."* [online] Goodreads.com. Available at: https://www.goodreads.*com*/quotes/248476-the-day-the-power-of-love-overrules-the-love-of
Truth, Sojourner., (n.d.). *"Truth is power, and it prevails."* [online] brainyquotes.com. Available at: https://www.brainyquote.com/quotes/sojourner_truth_380639, accessed October 21, 2022.

What time is it?
The acceptable time…Now
Lennon, John, McCartney, Paul., 1969. *Because* [online] wikipedia.org. Available at: https://en.wikipedia.org/wiki/Because_(Beatles_song)

Treading deep water?
Seek the meek connection
Ashford, Nickolas, Ross, Diana, Simpson, Valerie., 1970. *Reach Out and Touch (Somebody's Hand)* [online] wikipedia.org. Available at: https://en.wikipedia.org/wiki/Reach_Out_and_Touch_(Somebody%27s_Hand)

Broken Record or Not…
Jones, Lewis E., 1899. *Power in the Blood* [online] Hymnary.org. Available at: https://hymnary.org/text/would_you_be_free_from_the_burden_jones

The Nature of Grace
Three Dog Night., 1969, *Easy To Be Hard.* [online] SongLyrics.com. Available at: https://www.songlyrics.com/3-dog-night/easy-to-be-hard-lyrics/

Palms Up

Ketcham, Hank., 1951. *Dennis, the Menace.* [online] Fantagraphics.com. Available at: https://www.fantagraphics.com

Everywhere I go I feel love…

(Author Unknown)., (n.d), *Deep and Wide.* [online] Hymnal.net. Available at: https://www.hymnal.net/en/hymn/c/12
Crosby, Fanny., (n.d), *Blessed Assurance.* [online] Hymnary.org. Available at: https://hymnary.org/text/blessed_assurance_jesus_is_mine

Hope in the Heights

Sinatra, Frank., 1959. *High Hopes.* [online] Genius.com. Available at: https://genius.com/Frank-sinatra-high-hopes-lyrics

Sam and Dave., 1966. *Hold on, I'm Comin'.* [online] Genius.com. Available at: https://genius.com/Sam-and-dave-hold-on-im-comin-lyrics

For This Reason

Powell, Mac., 2021. *Love is the Reason.* [online] Multitracks.com. Available at: https://www.multitracks.com/songs/Mac-Powell/New-Creation/Love-Is-The-Reason/

"That'll Be the Day"

The Cowboy Way., 1994. [film] Director Champion, Greg. Vista de la Paz, Arroyo Seca, New Mexico, USA Universal Pictures

Bastian, Larry, Berghoff, Ed, Brooks, Garth., 1989. *Cowboy.* [online] Azlyrics.com. Available at: https://www.azlyrics.com/lyrics/garthbrooks/cowboybill.html
Holly, Buddy., 1957. *That'll Be the Day.* [online] Genius.com. Available at: https://genius.com/Buddy-holly-thatll-be-the-day-lyrics

Sealed with a Kiss

Geld, Gary, Udell, Peter, Vinton, Bobby., 1962/1972. *Sealed With a Kiss* [online] Azlyrics.com. Available at:
https://www.azlyrics.com/lyrics/bobbyvinton/sealedwithakiss.html
(Author Unknown)., (n.d.). Pentecost [online] Drivethruhistory.com. Available at:
https://drivethruhistory.com/history-of-pentecost/ Biblegateway.com. Available at:
https://www.biblegateway.com/quicksearch/?quicksearch=Pentecost&version=NIV

Let It Rain…

Jesus Culture., 2010. *Let It Rain.* [online] Azlyrics.com. Available at:
https://www.azlyrics.com/lyrics/jesusculture/letitrain.html

What the World Needs Now…

Owens, Grace W., 1926. *O Who Can Make a Flower* [online] Hymnary.org. Available at:
https://hymnary.org/text/o_who_can_make_a_flower
Knapp, Jacob., 1845. *Give Me Jesus* [online] Googlebooks.com. Available at:
https://www.google.com/books/edition/The_Evangelical_Harp/NAJMAAAAYAAJ?hl=en&gbpv=0

Whatsoever…

Top Gun Maverick., 2022. [film] Director Kosinski, Joseph. San Diego, California, USA
Top Gun., 1986. [film] Director Scott, Tony. Oceanside, California, USA
Loggins, Kenny., 1986. *Danger Zone.* [online] Genius.com. Available at:
https://genius.com/Kenny-loggins-danger-zone-lyrics

The Divine Dance
Khan, Chaka, Rufus, Wonder, Stevie., 1974. *Tell Me Something Good* [online] Azlyrics.com. Available at: https://www.azlyrics.com/lyrics/rufus/tellmesomethinggood.html
Lewis, C.S., 1942. *Mere Christianity* [online] Archive.org. Available at: https://archive.org/details/merechristianity0000csle/mode/2up?q=static and https://archive.org/details/merechristianity0000csle/page/136/mode/2up?q=fountain+

Basic Instructions Before Leaving Earth
Sons of the Desert., 1933. *Well, here's another nice mess you've gotten me into!* [film] Director Seiter, William. A., Spoken by: Hardy, Oliver.
The Rascals., 1968. *A Beautiful Morning.* [online] Azlyrics.com. Available at: https://www.azlyrics.com/lyrics/rascals/abeautifulmorning.html

Lead me kindly light…
Newman, John Henry., 1833. *Lead Me, Kindly Light, Amid the Encircling Gloom.* [online] Hymnary.org. Available at: https://hymnary.org/text/lead_kindly_light_amid_the_encircling_gl

Step and Fetch
Dorsey, Tommy., 1945. *On the Sunny Side of the Street.* [online] Azlyrics.biz. Available at: https://azlyrics.biz/t/tommy-dorsey-lyrics/tommy-dorsey-on-the-sunny-side-of-the-street-lyrics/
It's a Wonderful Life., 1946. [film] Director Capra, Frank. Culver City, California, USA.

Truth or Dare?
Lost in Space., 1965-68. *Danger, Will Robinson!* [television] Producer Allen, Irwin Spoken by The Robot.

Space is opportunity…In the blink of an eye…

Como, Perry, Sigman, Carl., 1956. *Dream Along With Me.* [online] Azlyrics.com. Available at: https://www.azlyrics.com/lyrics/perrycomo/dreamalongwithmeimonmywaytoastar.html
Thompson, Will Lamartine., 1880. *Softly and Tenderly Jesus is Calling.* [online] Hymnary.org. Available at: https://hymnary.org/text/softly_and_tenderly_jesus_is_calling
Moody, Dwight Lyman., 1837-1899. 'Will, I would rather have written "Softly and Tenderly Jesus Is Calling" than anything I have been able to do in my whole life.'' [online] Umcdiscipleship.org. Available at: https://www.umcdiscipleship.org/resources/history-of-hymns-softly-and-tenderly-jesus-is-calling

Shake, Rattle and Roll…Shall We Dance?

Calhoun, Charles, Presley, Elvis., 1955. *Shake, Rattle, and Roll.* [online] Genius.com. Available at: https://genius.com/Elvis-presley-shake-rattle-and-roll-lyrics

The Nitty Gritty… "Listen to your life"

Buechner, Fredrick., (n.d.). *Listen to your life.* [online] Goodreads.com. Available at: https://www.goodreads.com/quotes/158523-listen-to-your-life-see-it-for-the-fathomless-mystery

Mixed Messages… "Choose you this day…"

Gogh, Vincent Van., (n.d.). *Conscience is a man's compass.* [online] Quotefancy.com. Available at: https://quotefancy.com/quote/927871/Vincent-van-Gogh-Conscience-is-a-man-s-compass-and-though-the-needle-sometimes-deviates

3 Little Birds on Granny's Path

The United Church of Canada., 1968. *A New Creed*. [online] The United Church of Canada. Available at: https://united-church.ca/community-faith/welcome-united-church-canada/faith-statements/new-creed-1968

Marley, Bob., 1977. *Three Little Birds*. [online] Azlyrics.com Available at: https://www.azlyrics.com/lyrics/bobmarley/threelittlebirds.html

Sad Eyes…Open the Floodgates of Heaven

Elizabeth, Queen II., 2016. *Queen's Christmas Message*. [online] Bbc.com. Available at: https://www.bbc.com/news/uk-38427380

To Blame is Lame…Rather, Exclaim the Name!

Sons of the Desert., 1933. *Well, here's another nice mess you've gotten me into!* [film] Director Seiter, William. A., Spoken by: Hardy, Oliver.

Leonard, Tasha Cobbs, Reagan, Will., 2013. *Break Every Chain*. [online] Azlyrics.com. Available at: https://www.azlyrics.com/lyrics/tashacobbs/breakeverychain.html

The "Wrong" Stuff vs. The "Right Stuff"

Neuhaus, Richard John., 1979. *Freedom For Ministry*. [online] Googlebooks.com. Available at: https://www.google.com/books/edition/Freedom_for_Ministry/W23Hb4a3thYC?hl=en&gbpv=0

Neuhaus, Richard John., (n.d.). *In the absence of truth, power is the only game in town*. [online] Azquotes.com. Available at: https://www.azquotes.com/quote/531082

Walk it, Talk it in Your Heart -Then, Come Home … Softly and Tenderly

Lathrap, Mary Torrans., 1898. *Walk a mile in his moccasins*. [online]Libertyandprosperity.com. Available at: https://libertyandprosperity.com/judge-softly-walk-a-mile-in-his-moccasins-by-mary-t-lathrap-1895/

When "Lest" is "More"
Blanchard, Richard., 19. *Fill My Cup, Lord* [online] Hymnary.org. Available at:
https://hymnary.org/text/fill_my_cup_lord_i_lift_it_up_lord

Wound Care…Beyond Band-Aids
Cohen, Leonard., 1992. *Anthem* [online] Azlyrics.com. Available at:
https://www.azlyrics.com/lyrics/leonardcohen/anthem.html

The "Joy" Road and The 4 "R's"
Steinbeck, John., 1939. *The Grapes of Wrath* [online] Wikipedia.org. Available at:
https://en.wikipedia.org/wiki/The_Grapes_of_Wrath

Not if, but when...Some things are certain
Rusthoi, Esther Kerr., 1941. *When We See Christ* [online] Hymnary.org. Available at:
https://hymnary.org/text/oft_times_the_day_seems_long

References Editor

Kathern Lynn Harless is an editor/writer of both fiction and non-fiction born in Oslo, Norway in 1969. Being raised in a military family, they moved every time her dad received his orders, hence her being born abroad. For the better part of 40 years Kathern has called Memphis home; she lives in the heart of Memphis, Normal Station Neighborhood, with her son Andrew and daughter Ellen, along with their Fox Hound pup Brandi. Ms. Harless' writing tends to lean towards the human condition. She has the uncanny ability to make your heart swell, shatter it to pieces, and melt the tiny shards with the stroke of her pen. In March of 2018, she made her literary debut as a contributing writer in *The Collection: Flash Fiction for Flash Memory* with the story *A Good Left Hook*.

For inquire information about Kathern Lynn Harless and her editing and writing services: (harlesseditingservices.com) and (https://medium.com/@kathernharless).

Contributing Writer - Steve Canfield - *Abba*

After graduating from Bible College with a degree in Bible and counseling, Steve served as a youth pastor in Illinois. Since joining Life Action Ministries in 1975, he has communicated family- centered, revival-oriented truths to over a million people in churches, camps, public high schools, and civic auditoriums. Debby faithfully serves alongside her husband. They have committed their lives believing God for nationwide revival.

Artists

Featured Artist: Daniel Bonnell

Mary in Her Ninth Month, Deposition of Compassion, Seascape

My painting reflects on the ultimate human need to fulfill an intrinsic longing that extends from birth to death. Simply put, it is a need to be held. My art symbolically speaks to this notion, especially with darkness (black) embracing light (color), with negative space enclosing positive space, I paint primarily on grocery bag paper with mis-tinted house paint. In my process this surface is surrogate for human skin that reflects life, especially so, when the heavy paper is saturated with pigments, oils, wax, and fragrances. The concept of using something that was once a utilitarian container also speaks to the theme of being held. My latest paintings follow a path wherein they are recycled back into yet another painting, as is they were sacrificing itself for a greater work. The painting is never finished, it is only at rest. Such a process is known as kenosis, or purging of the essence within each painting to create a greater work of art. This process is born out of contemplative thought and writings of the mystics. Working on modest surfaces with humble means permits this direction in a very natural manner. My paintings become a creative conductor that allows me to be held.

Maria Hunt – *The Sabbath* (Title Page Art), *God's Love Note*

"Art, something I always wanted as part of my life, has become a passion that fills my soul, and leaves me full of joy, one brushstroke at a time." After 30 years as a successful business woman, my husband and I retired to the Palm Springs area, where I pursued her childhood dream of studying and creating art. I started in 2000 with art classes at College of the Desert, refining my skills in plein air painting by attending workshops across the U.S. My love for my Creator, and His creations, is evident in all my artwork. More recently, I used my talent to raise funds for various charities in the desert (Actual "Antique Pages" from my husband's grandfather's "Cyclopedias," printed in 1884, which provide the basis for participants to create their own works of art to take home and the class fee is contributed directly to the charity. (Go to Maria-Hunt.Pixels.com to see the art participants create in the "Art on Antique Pages gallery) Since 2013 I have donated a weekly, relaxing hour or so of fun to the mothers in crisis pregnancies at "Mama's House, for women avoiding abortions.

(Go to https://www.themamashouse.org to learn more about their life-saving efforts. You can contact me at mariahunt@mindspring.com or, online at Maria-Hunt.Pixels.com to view my artwork.

Featured Music Arranger and Musician

 Hailed by the Memphis Commercial Appeal as a "teenage virtuoso," Basil Alter is a violinist from Memphis. Currently based in New York, he is a student at Manhattan School of Music studying violin. As a classical concert violinist, he has performed nationally and internationally to great acclaim. In addition, he is a featured performer on albums from a wide array of genres. Outside of performing, he is a sought-after music arranger and music transcriber for artists across the globe. He has been featured in the University of Memphis Magazine, WKNO FM's "Checking In on the Arts," and Jewish Scene Magazine. In the rare moments where he is not working on something musical he can be found doing the New York Times daily crossword. He is grateful to Lana Lee Marler, author of *Heaven's Peace Reflections,* for inviting him and giving him the opportunity to complete the musical arrangements for her. Please visit his website: basilalter.com .

All music for this publication, Heaven's Peace Reflections, was professionally recorded at the historic Sam Phillips Recording Studio in Memphis, Tennessee, Scott Bomar – Engineer.

Featured Musicians

 Classical guitarist, Michelle Shrader focused on vocal training, competing vocally and performing hundreds of concerts before the age of twelve and became interested in guitar at the age of fifteen. After moving to Memphis in 2006 to study classical guitar with Lily Afshar, she fell in love with the city and stayed after the completion of her degree in 2013. Michelle is now a popular fixture in the local music scene singing jazz and guitar selections for private events at various Memphis venues. She has also been featured in local media for her songwriting. Michelle carries a private teaching studio, owns Music for Aardvarks Memphis and particularly enjoys developing youthful talent. Above all else, she wishes to spread her love for music to others in the community.

Vocalist

Lana Lee Marler, singer/song writer and author of three books, including Heaven's Peace Reflections, is the featured vocalist on all music recordings in this book.

Music

Heaven's Peace

Lyrics by Lana Lee Marler, PDM Music by C. Hubert H. Parry (1916); arr. Basil Alter; Guitar - Michelle Shrader; Vocal - Lana Lee Marler

The Longing

Lyrics and Music by Lana Lee Marler, arr. Basil Alter; Guitar-Michelle Shrader; Vocal - Lana Lee Marler

Even So, Come

Lyrics and Music by Lana Lee Marler; arr. Basil Alter; Guitar- Michelle Shrader; Vocal - Lana Lee Marler

Prayer to the Holy Spirit

Traditional Native American Prayer, Translated by Lakota Sioux Chief Yellow Lark (1887), Music by Lana Lee Marler, arr. Basil Alter; Vocal-Lana Lee Marler

Epiphany

Lyrics and Music by Lana Lee Marler; arr. Basil Alter; Guitar-Michelle Shrader; Vocal - Lana Lee Marler

Surrender

Lyrics by Lana Lee Marler, PDM Music- *Coventry Carol* (Traditional Carol), arr. Basil Alter; Guitar-Michelle Shrader; Vocal - Lana Lee Marler

The Beauty of Your Love

Lyrics by Lana Lee Marler, PDM Music – *Eventide* by William Henry Monk (1861); arr. and Violin Basil Alter; Guitar-Michelle Shrader; Vocal - Lana Lee Marler

O Breath of Life

PDM Lyrics by Bessie Porter Head (1920) and Music by Lana Lee Marler; arr. Basil Alter; Vocal - Lana Lee Marler

The Wishing Well

Lyrics adapted by Connie Dover from the poem, *Renunciation* by Padraic Pearse; Music by Connie Dover, Additional Lyrics and Music by Lana Lee Marler; arr. Basil Alter; Violin-Basil Alter; Guitar-Michelle Shrader; Vocal - Lana Lee Marler

Back to the Garden

Lyrics and Music by Lana Lee Marler; Vocal - Lana Lee Marler

Any Day Now

PDM Music – *Londonderry Air* (Traditional Irish Melody); Lyrics by Lana Lee Marler; Vocal - Lana Lee Marler

God's Love Note
A Testimony
by
Maria Hunt

I was lost in prayer, in a parking lot with cars coming and going. "Father, **please** help me the next couple of days. I am in pain and at my wits end." I approached my friend's car and set down the box of groceries to open the trunk. And there, inches from my feet, was a leaf... with a **Heart** at its center - broken pieces of the leaf forming it perfectly. "Oh," I cried to my friend, "It's a **Love Note from God!**"

How instant was God's response...He let me know in the most artistic way that He heard me. Needless to say, the next two days were **miraculous!**

Is it interesting to you that an artist found the leaf? The story is *old and new; told and retold,* reminding us that God is a prayer away... **Always.**

Abba
by Steve Canfield

Though He is our Master,
Potentate and King;
Sustainer and Creator,
Lord of everything.

Deserving all our honor,
Before Him humbly bowed;
Bound by grace and mercy,
To Him forever vowed.

Yet when we come before Him,
His hand outstretched to ours,
He bids us call him Father,
As He tends our sinful scars.

There is no condemnation,
In love He does caress;
And hold us as His child,
In joy and in distress.

"And because you are sons, God has sent the Spirit of his Son into our hearts, crying, 'Abba! Father!'" Galatians 4:6

About the Author

Lana Lee Marler offers her third book in this weekly resource of meditations and music for the Liturgical Calendar Year. Her first two books were entitled: Follow Me – A Seasonal Journey, published in 2017 and Cast Your Net Again...For Such a Time as This, published in 2022. Lana is a poet, singer/song writer, and church music director. A wife and mother, she is partner in ministry with her husband who is a United Methodist minister. Lana is an artist in any medium, but long ago chose music to express her relationship to God. Her faith journey led her to a major in sacred music in college and has crossed the landscape of three denominations: Baptist, Methodist and Episcopal. Spending countless hours mastering the hymnody and liturgies of these quite varied traditions has added depth and richness to her Christian perspective. Moreover, her musical DNA is infused with the music of the times in which she grew up- – the 1960's. Whether the song is Joan Baez's "Swing Low" or "Just As I Am" sung from a back row Baptist pew, she connects with each tradition in authenticity. In 2004, Lana and her husband, Rev. William D. Marler, co-founded Jacob's LadderTM Community Development Corporation, a non-profit charity serving inner-city Memphis, where the Gospel of Christ is shared through community building, housing rehabilitation and education. All proceeds from this book will go to benefit the communities served by Jacob's LadderTM (jacobsladdercdc.org)

Printed in the United States
by Baker & Taylor Publisher Services